Help!
They're all out to get me!

The motorcyclists guide to surviving the everyday world

By Ralph L. Angelo Jr.

Help! They're All Out to Get Me!
The Motorcyclists Guide to Surviving the Everyday World

Cover Photo: Ralph L. Angelo, Jr. Riding on Rte. 112 in Massachusetts, Courtesy Mike Stefansen.

Dedication

This book is dedicated to first my riding buddies who I learned so much from in the early years, and who I continue to enjoy and savor every moment of riding with up to today and beyond! Mike, Jerry, Paul, Dave, George, Diane, Robert, Bill and everyone else in the LIMELongriders.org, as well as Dave P. and Ken C. Up in New England!

Secondly, and more importantly this goes out to my family Rick, Ronnie, Robbie, Mom, and Dad and to my somewhat adopted brothers Joel and Chris! You guys are all the best! Without any of you, none of this would ever have happened. Joel, if you hadn't have walked into that dealership with me that day, I would still not be on a motorcycle. Thank you! Chris, even though you're not involved in riding anymore, we had great times while you were. Mom and Dad, you two are the best! Without you I would not have become who I am. Rick, Ronnie and Robbie, my younger brothers, one of these days I'll get you guys on bikes, and you'll see what you've been missing! I love you all, Thanks!

I also want to send a very special thank you to my buddy Jerry Zuckerman for all his help editing and rereading this book for me over the months. Thanks man, I couldn't have done it without you!

And lastly, on a more somber note, this book is dedicated to my longtime friend, one of the very best buddies a guy could ever have, who left us all at a far, far too young age in life, Fred McGloine. I miss you Freddie. I wish I could have gotten you on a motorcycle in the short time you had on this Earth, you would have enjoyed it immensely, but in general I just miss you. God bless you, my friend.

Ralph

Preface:

What is this book about you may ask? Why was it even written? Good questions, grasshopper. And they are ones I intend to answer, to your everlasting regret! (Well I hope not at least!)

Here's the deal: This book is about survival when the motorcyclist is faced with his greatest enemy, the four-wheeled driver. Four wheelers routinely cut us off, run us over, pull into our lanes, and generally, are just out to get us.

Or so it may seem. It's actually not THAT bad, but it is best to think that way, and to always be prepared for the worst.

This is where this book and I come in. This book is going to teach you all the little tricks and nuances that I've learned in over 200,000 crash free miles in the past 18 years. Who am I to be teaching anyone anything? Well, I'm just a guy who rides sport bikes real far every year. I own a '98 Yamaha YZF600R and a '95 Kawasaki GPZ1100, as well as a '01 Kawasaki W650 and a '06 Yamaha FJR1300 and between them, I ride a lot of miles a year. I learned on a "proper sized" motorcycle, my first bike, a brand spanking new '94 Yamaha Seca II that was a left over in '95, and I put almost 40,000 miles on that baby, before graduating to something a LOT faster and better handling. I am also a contributor to such magazines as "Motorcycle Consumer News (MCN)," "Backroads Motorcycle Tour magazine", and "Motorcycle Online" (Motorcycle.com).

So before you start saying, "Hey, this guy has no credentials to teach us anything!" Think a second, 200,000+ crash free miles has to count for something, right? Give me a chance here, and I think you will find yourself learning and enjoying a few things along the way to enlightenment, oh celestial two wheeler-o-phile! I'm also a New York State Certified Motorcycle Instructor, so that has to count right?

Also, this book is written differently than others you may have read, because I'm going to be talking to you as if we were old friends. The reading will be light, and enjoyable (I hope!)

So pull up a chair, sit back, and have fun!

Contents

Chapter One 1
Chapter Two 9
Chapter Three 17
Chapter Four 24
Chapter Five 29
Chapter Six 33
Chapter Seven 37
Chapter Eight 41
Chapter Nine 47
Chapter Ten 52
Chapter Eleven 58
Chapter Twelve 65
Chapter Thirteen 73
Chapter Fourteen 76
Chapter Fifteen 80
Chapter Sixteen 82
Chapter Seventeen 85
Chapter Eighteen 89
Chapter Nineteen 91
Chapter Twenty 96
Chapter Twenty One 100
Chapter Twenty Two 109

Chapter Twenty Three 119
Chapter Twenty Four 124
Chapter Twenty Five 127
Chapter Twenty Six 132
Chapter Twenty Seven 138
Chapter Twenty Eight 143
Chapter Twenty Nine 146
Chapter Thirty 151
Chapter Thirty One 153
Chapter Thirty Two 155
Appendix 159
Final thoughts 165

Chapter One

So where do you start with a book about surviving the everyday dangers of motorcycling? Why at the beginning of course! And what exactly does that mean? It means even if you are an old hand at this, you're going to have to sit through a few things you might-or might not know already.

So let's begin at the beginning then. What is this thing called Motorcycling? Real simple, grasshopper. It is more than a hobby, and less than a reason for living, though some would argue that comment as well. Motorcycling gets in your blood. It can make you become crazed and vision centered all at once. Your motorcycle(s) become your friends, your girlfriends, and your constant companion at times. Or they can just become a vehicle to carry you quickly and conveniently to and from work or school or wherever you need to be.

So what does all that mean? Not a whole hell of a lot, depending on who you talk to. Though others will say it is a mantra to live by.

In a nutshell: Motorcycling will provide you with untold years of enjoyment, as well as new friends. It will make you sit up at night reading all about it (Like from this book.) As well as make you sit around for months beforehand planning out trips everywhere you can. It doesn't much matter what size bike you ride, (I have heard of Iron Butt participants doing rides on 250 cc machines. What's an "Iron Butt"? I'll get to that later on.) Just as long as you ride, and ride the right way.

What does the right way mean? It means

don't ride like the guys you see on cable TV shows who build so-called "Custom Choppers", helmet less and wearing only a leather vest and fingerless gloves. You may be saying "Yeah, but they look cool and that's what I want out of motorcycling." If that's the case then throw this book away now, and go get yourself one of those useless beanies the cruiser guys wear.

Still here? Good. Now you're going to learn the right way to ride.

So what is the right way to ride? Better to ask what is the right preparation to ride, right? Easy answer. Get yourself a full face DOT/Snell approved helmet, a pair of good quality riding gloves, a good Motorcycle quality armored jacket (Either leather or Cordura is the way to go. And no, the denim jacket you've been wearing the last four years is NOT protection for a motorcycle ride.) Also a good pair of riding pants are a necessity for riding the right way.

Make sure whatever your choices are for body protection includes armor. Next up is boots. Make sure they are M/C (Motorcycle) specific, and not just an old pair of Uncle Bill's work boots. You can get either waterproof or non-waterproof. High cut (Almost up to the knee) or mid cut (Above the ankle), which ever you prefer. If you don't need boots that are specifically water proof, you can always invest in a pair of boot gaiters, to keep your feet dry in times of thunderstorms and the like.

Notice I talked about protective gear first? There's a reason. If you can't afford the right gear, then you shouldn't be thinking about getting a bike. Time to prioritize, speed racer. Riding gear is what protects your skin, in case of contact with the pavement. I know I would rather have a thick layer of 1000 denier Cordura between the tar roadway and me any day of the week. Do you think shorts and an Oakley T-shirt riding up your back at eighty miles per hour are proper riding gear? Think again. Most guys who ride like that are also the ones who take the most chances when riding. You see them zipping in and out of traffic, and lane splitting as well as doing the 'stoopid' stunts like wheelies and stoppies and all the other things that give motorcyclists a bad name. (Wait until you get to chapter 8!)

So what are the differences in riding gear materials? Well, leather has been used for years. Good ol' cowhide has some good properties when it comes to protecting YOUR hide. But there are many different degrees of leather. Some are just too thin for motorcycle use. These are the store bought or designer leathers you find in your local mall's leather shop. These are not good for Motorcycle use. Brands like Joe Rocket, First Gear, Gericke, AGV, Vanson, Alpinestars, and many more produce motorcycle grade and motorcycle specific jackets and pants in heavy leather that is made just for motorcycling. These jackets and pants also include armor of varying types.

Other manufacturers use a material called Cordura, which is a Dupont product. Cordura is a nylon type of thread, which varies in degrees of thickness based on a manufacturer's usage. Some use 600 denier (Denier is the measurement of thickness for Cordura.) Others use 1000 denier. The higher the denier, the better. These suits also use a form of armor, depending on the manufacturer. The thicker the armor, the obviously better. Companies like Motoport, Aerostitch, First Gear, Joe Rocket, Gericke, AGV and many more all make Cordura riding apparel. Do your own exhaustive research into these, and see what fits you best, both wallet-wise and usage-wise. The minimum denier I would recommend personally is 600. There are some manufacturers who use only 320 denier on their riding gear, and I wouldn't touch that. The higher the denier, the better.

 Armor in all these suits should be positioned in the hips, the back, the knees, the shoulders, the arms, and the chest. Something that has armor in the collarbone area is especially helpful, because this seems to be the most common bone to break for a motorcyclist.

 The Cordura suits come either waterproof or can be made such with a zip in lining. This is the preferred style. The waterproof suits do not breathe, and in the heat of summer becomes a liability. It's a good idea to get a suit (Jacket and pants combo, or one piece) that breathes.

 A relatively new phenomenon is the mesh style jacket that almost all the major manufacturers are making these days. These all have one form or another of armor within them, and are free flowing for very hot weather use. I myself own a Joe Rocket Phoenix jacket, as well as an optional waterproof/thinsulate lined lining. These things are great products that work. While they absolutely do NOT give you the protection of a 3/4 length Cordura jacket or a leather jacket, they offer more than adequate protection, especially when compared with wearing a T-shirt. It's a much more desirable option to saying, "It's too hot to wear a jacket."

Another good option to consider is the Kevlar jeans being marketed by several companies these days. While it is far more preferable to wear good quality Cordura or leather riding pants, most sport riders do tend to ride in jeans. The Kevlar style jean will NOT burn through, and will save your hide from being burned and torn up. There is even optional armor available for them, which is even better. These are acceptable for local riding, but offer no impact protection like Cordura pants with armor do. Only the optional armor will help out in these cases.

Helmets are the single most important piece of equipment you can own. They protect your brain, and your face. Just remember, on all head impacts in a crash, you have a one in four chance of landing on your face. I have seen face shields where people have slid face first on the pavement. There is nothing left of them. That could very well have been flesh hitting the pavement. Don't let anyone fool you into thinking it's not manly or cool to wear a full face helmet. It's far smarter and cooler to have that full face on tightly when and if you go down, then to be wearing a beanie helmet, which is totally useless. You'll get back up, even with a little hospital stay if need be, but the other guy might not. The other guy will be hideously disfigured and require months, sometimes years of reconstructive surgery to approximate what he looked like prior to his accident, that is if he isn't brain damaged or outright dead from head trauma. Arai, Shoei, AGV, KBC, HJC, Nolan, Suomy and many more helmet manufacturers have first rate helmets to protect your most important attribute, your brain. Go see what fits you best. My only recommendation here is getting one that is both DOT and SNELL certified.

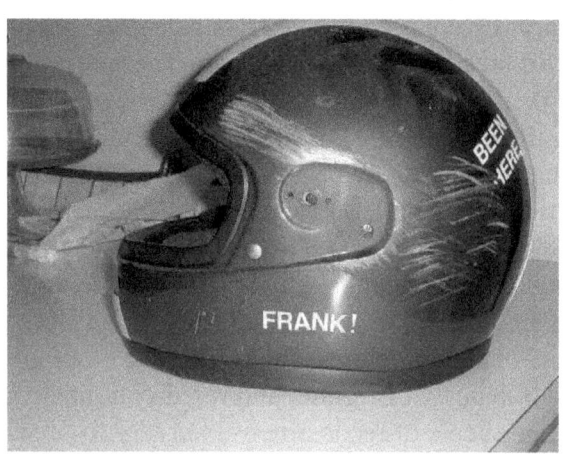

Next question you have is what are DOT and SNELL, and what do they mean? DOT stands for Department Of Transportation, and SNELL is actually the last name of someone in whose honor a helmet testing service was started. The SNELL tests are by far the most comprehensive, and the DOT tests are actually very vague from what I've been able to discern. So to be safe I would purchase a helmet that is certified by both organizations.

Just a note on helmets, don't let anyone tell you that you need less than a full-face helmet. Just recently, a rock skipped up from a car's tire, and smacked me right in the middle of my face shield. If I had been wearing a cruiser style beanie, I would have been hurt badly enough to lose control of the motorcycle and crash. There's absolutely no doubt in my mind of that.

Gloves are another issue altogether. There are literally thousands of different types available. Perforated, gel impregnated, gauntlets, full race, waterproof, the list goes on and on. Tour master,

Olympia, Alpinestars and many others are the manufacturers of choice. Get out there and try them on, see what fits, and what works best for you. Obviously the thicker the glove, the better the protection. When I travel, I carry three different types of glove with me at least. A perforated, a thinly insulated middle weight, and a waterproof, or a winter waterproof. Find what works best for you, and then put it to use.

We're very blessed in this post 20th century era to have ultra-modern technologies at our disposal to aid us in surviving on the street as every day motorcyclists! We just have to be smart enough to use them.

Chapter Two

So what should you ride? That's the burning question on your ever so feverish mind, eh oh inquisitive one? Well I'm here to tell you, you should ride something that has low power, good brakes, and be light enough to gain confidence on, at least for the first year or two (Preferably two at least.)

When beginning as a new rider, you should really consider something with no more than 50 horsepower. Now I know you've been looking at that shiny new R1, GSXR1000 or CBR1000, but I'm here to tell you, you are making a big mistake considering one of those bad boys this early in your riding career. In all seriousness, if you are really considering a full on sport bike, especially a Liter "Superbike" your mistake could actually be life ending, so think before you sign on the dotted line. I've heard, and seen to many people roll out of the dealership on something way to powerful for their nascent hands, and end up laying in the street with their brand new bikes, no more than a scant few minutes later.

Now let me put it to you this way: really, the very best thing you can do when first learning to ride, is to buy a used bike of small power and displacement. Hands down, this is the best choice you can make. I know, I know, you think you're a man and you can handle anything. Well guess what? It's time to be honest with yourself and admit you don't know everything. Getting your feet wet on something you won't have a total coronary over when you drop it (And I hate to say it, but there's a good chance you will drop it. Nothings definite, but why take a chance?) So what I'm going to do here is give you my choices for a first bike with the pluses and minuses. You can take it from there.

1) Yamaha Seca II 600 CC's Manufactured from 92-98 with an air cooled, easy to work on motor that makes about 50 HP. Nice handling bike that builds confidence, and has almost no plastic to break when dropped. Comfortable, wide seat. Rock solid and fun to ride, whether long distance or locally, the Seca II is a bike you can live with for many years. A Lightweight at 406 Lbs. dry, with a 4.5 gallon gas tank.

2) Suzuki Bandit 600 All of the above, plus more power. More than adequate wind protection. Poorly designed seat needs to be replaced for most, though.

Excellent first choice as well. 31.1" seat height could be a problem for those of the low inseam set. 5.3 gallon tank is major plus.

3) Honda Nighthawk 650. Been around since the mid '80's. A maintenance free bike, basically. Shaft drive and hydraulic lifters are both major pluses. Down side is the *much* too small gas tank (3.4 gal.)

4) Suzuki GS500 a small, naked twin Suzuki has produced for years. Practical (Not a dirty word!) And a perfect beginner bike. 5.3 gallon tank is MASSIVE for a bike of this size. This bike has been around since '89, so there are many examples out there, looking to be ridden.

5) Kawasaki EX500/500 Ninja. This is a great beginner's bike that is basically bulletproof. Twin 500cc bike that has been in production since the late '80's. The bike produces 54 horsepower, along with its very light weight of 388 Lbs. make this entry level bike another perfect choice for beginners. 30.5" seat height is also about an inch lower than current sport bikes.

6) Kawasaki ZR7S a recent faired bike that has a 5.8 Gallon tank, as well as roomy ergoes and a sporting pedigree make this a perfect choice for a first bike. At 463 lbs. dry, it's a little porky, but still very manageable. This one has the largest motor of the lot, a 738 cc in line four. The 31.5" seat height is again, a little tall for some. Based on Kawasaki's powerful and bulletproof designs, this bike is a great

beginner's choice.

7) Yamaha V-Star 650.This is a bike that will not get you into trouble on your beginner-riding trek. Very low HP as well as equally low seat height (28") makes for a comfortable and unchallenging first bike, if you're into cruisers. Gas tank size is a little anemic (4.25 gals.) And the weight is slightly hefty (505 Lbs.) But all in all it's a great bike to start on.

There are others to choose from, but those are motorcycles that you will outgrow very quickly, usually in a few months. They are all small motorcycles with either one cylinder or very little displacement, which are great to learn on, but not much else. The ones I mentioned above will last you several seasons before you gain the itch to buy something new. Furthermore, you should ride a motorcycle like I mentioned above for at the very least a year or hopefully two to get yourself accustomed to riding. A motorcycle like these helps to build confidence and experience for the nascent rider.

These examples above are all relatively recent motorcycles, which should be available in large quantities on the market. There are more bikes out there that will suit your needs, but these will all be older, and as such, mechanically archaic. Stay away from something that does not have electronic ignition. Also motorcycles that old tend to have things dried up and in need of replacement, such as hoses and various seals. Low mileage is not a good thing either. If you come upon a bike that has 10,000 miles on the clock and it is twenty years old, I would walk away immediately. It is NOT a good thing. Better to buy a motorcycle that has been ridden and maintained then one that has sat around for the past five plus years getting rusty. A motorcycle like this will cost you a helluva lot in maintenance just to get it roadworthy.

    Now, speaking of maintenance, what does it take to get a new (To you) motorcycle roadworthy? Expect to spend some money. Don't fool yourself. You may need tires (Figure $200 plus mounting costs), brake pads ($40 per disk, if you have a three disk system, as most motorcycles do, figure $120), plus other things. You may need light bulbs for various lights, including dashboard lights. If you need a chain and sprockets, and do the work yourself, figure you're still going to be in for $150+ in parts. If you have someone else do the replacement, add another $100 at least. Always do at least an oil and filter change to start off with if the bike needs nothing else. Be aware that there are plenty of other things that could happen when you buy a used bike, and must be prepared for. So make sure you have some money in reserve, just in case you have this eventuality. Just bear in mind to thoroughly check out whatever you decide to buy.

    What should you look for? Starting at the front of the bike, look at the fork seals, which are the round rings on each fork where the sections slide into each other. If you see any amount of oil on the sliding sections, or see oil dripping down the legs, the bike needs fork seals. Make sure you factor that into the offer you'll make for the bike. It's going to cost you close to $300 to have those seals replaced.

Now go to the steering stem and if the bike has a center stand, put the bike on the center stand, rock it back onto the rear tire, and have someone pull the front rim back and forth to look for steering head play. If there is play, the head bearings will need to be either tightened, or replaced. Another expensive proposition that should be taken into consideration.

Now turn the bike on. Start it, and note how it feels when first started. Is it smooth? Or very rough? It shouldn't be too rough, if it is, and stays that way during warm up, then you might have some other type of problem in the engine there as well. Don't confuse vibrations that all bikes make with just plain old running rough.

Now go to the chain. Roll the rear tire while on the center stand, or if no center stand is on the bike, roll the bike forward and listen to the chain, while checking it for tight spots and kinks, as well as rust and lack of oil. If this bike has any of those above problems, then you'll need a chain and sprockets (Always replace chain and sprockets together, never one without the other. The reason for this? Sprockets wear, and the teeth turn pointy as the chain gets older. If you replace just the chain, it will wear out prematurely.)

Now get on the ground, and look at the brake pads. See how thick they are. If they are paper thin, or even look like they are heading that way, realize they will have to be replaced. Make sure you check all the pads. As I said earlier there are anywhere from two to three rotors on any bike, and that means you have anywhere from two to three sets of pads.

    Check your cables next. Pull in the clutch cable (If not a hydraulic clutch.) And look for any fraying. If you see any at all, then the cable has to be replaced. Repeat the procedure with the throttle cables, if you can. Doing this involves removing the right throttle housing, and the current owner may not be too happy about pulling apart his throttle housing. If he says no, then just make sure you check it if you decide to buy the bike once you get it home. All cables need lubing annually, by the way, but we'll hit on annual maintenance later on.

    Now go to the rear shock or shocks. Push up and down on the seat, compressing the rear shock repeatedly. Does it go down to easily? Is there any type of resistance to your repeated shock compressions? If so, that's good. If the shock feels like a pogo stick, then you have problems there. New shocks can cost anywhere from $250-$1000, depending on what brand you buy.

    Look at the tires. Are they dry rotted? Is there tread left? Look for the wear bar indicators in the center of the tire, and see how close the tread is to the wear indicators. If the tires are dry rotted (Little cracks around the edges of the tire.) or the tread is getting close to the wear indicators, you know you'll have to immediately put tires on if you buy this bike.

    Okay, so the bike you're looking at has so far passed your test criteria. What next? Start it and run it. Making sure the bike doesn't puff blue smoke. If it does, walk away. You don't want to buy a motorcycle that you'll be adding oil to all the time.

Everything else looks okay? Then you're half way there. Make a deal for the best price you can with the soon to be previous owner, and be on your way.

Chapter Three

So you bought yourself a motorcycle and now riding gear as well (Preferably gear first then the bike!) And you don't know where you go from here, huh pilgrim? Well I can answer that for you. You pick up your phone book and look up your nearest MSF (Motorcycle Safety Foundation) rider's course. Now if you have previous experience, you take an experienced rider's course. If you don't then you take a beginner's rider's course.

You might even want to take the beginner's course before you buy a bike, as it will really let you know if this is for you or not. You don't have to be a motorcycle owner to take the course, and if you do pass it, you get your operator's license without having to take the DMV road test. If you fail it, you are allowed a retest a few weeks later. Also you can discover if you really want to do this. States vary on this so check it out with your nearest MSF provider.

Riding a motorcycle is not just something you do on a whim. Sure, most of us have started out that way, but you really have to think about how dangerous this is in the real world. I myself believe it's not as dangerous as others make it out to be, and that to succeed at this, you have to keep both eyes open and processing information on a continuous basis. To ride a motorcycle requires a steadfast commitment to do it right, and to not take the process lightly, because, and have no doubt about this; your life depends on <u>*YOU*</u> taking your riding seriously!

So what does all that gibberish I just said mean? It means eyes open, no distractions, check your mirrors constantly, and assume (and this is the big one!) That EVERYONE is out to get you! You have to ride like every driver out there does not see you, because chances are they do not. If you're new to motorcycling you haven't yet seen this written in your local paper, but when you begin to notice these things (And you will) the article will go something like this: "Motorcyclist killed in collision with car, Mrs. Smith made a left turn onto main St. and was hit in the side of her car by a motorcycle ridden by Mr. Jones."

Left hand turns by cars are the number one cause of death in motorcycle-car collisions. Cars continually turn left in front of motorcycles, and in that sort of scenario, you lose!

So what can be done to minimize your

chances of that type of an accident? (There are many other types, and we'll get into those, and why we're our own worst enemies later on!) You have to anticipate and process what is happening in front of you. When you see that car pulling up to that corner ahead of you, and you know she's going to make a left turn in front of you (Check out her tires, what direction are they pointed in? A lot of drivers DO NOT use their turn signals, so just because you do not see a left blinker on, does not mean she's not going to zip in front of you. Assume she is, and cover your brake levers, as well as your clutch, plan out your evasive action before you need it, and above all, lower your speed to something you can manage in case of emergency! Just remember, that driver could be on a very important Cell phone call to the bakery concerning her husband's birthday cake, and she may have no time to be concerned about her driving! If that's the case, and she is involved with something other than her driving, whether it be her kids on the back seat, or her make up in the mirror, she will pull out in front of you and whatever happens next, YOU will bear the brunt of! So slow it down in intersections, and be prepared for the worst.

But before we get too far ahead of ourselves, let's backtrack to the beginning, shall we? You are now a licensed rider. You bought a motorcycle after you received your license, and are now ready to hit the open road. By the open road you mean the coffee shop five miles from home. It's good to have a destination, and one not too far from home on a first ride is very important, so as not to spook yourself.

But did you know that most accidents happen within 4-5 miles of home? That's why it's also a good idea to have a more experienced, educated rider with you. One who believes in full gear and proper riding technique, so he can show you the ropes as it were. If your buddy wants to go to the bar, and routinely wears a leather vest and beanie helmet, find another riding buddy, period. Motorcycles and alcohol DO NOT MIX! I can't say that emphatically enough, but it is true. When you see all those motorcycles parked around a bar in the middle of the afternoon on Sunday, shake your head and keep on rolling.

So you're on your driveway, and about to go for your inaugural ride. You put in your ear plugs, (Yes, you heard me right, your ear plugs. Air rushing past your helmet at speed can irrevocably damage your hearing. So buy a box of them and use them every time you throw a leg over the seat. You'll soon realize you can't ride without them.) Put your helmet on, and tighten the chinstrap. Make sure you keep the chinstrap cinched up, because in case of an accident you don't want your helmet flying off. Now make sure your jacket is in place and zipped up. Tighten the wrist closures, and put on your gloves, tightening them up as well. Get on your bike. Set the choke (If not fuel injected) pull in the clutch, start it. Let it warm up a minute at least. Pull your face shield down, and roll slowly down your driveway into the street, while checking in both directions before you actually enter the roadway. Once out and rolling, keep your eyes flashing from side to side constantly as well as back to both mirrors. Know what's happening in front of you, as well as behind you at all times. Cover your brake levers constantly with full fingers, and begin to scan ahead.

What is scanning ahead? Imagine you have a bubble around your bike, of twelve seconds of time in all directions. It's your responsibility to keep those twelve seconds in view constantly. To know what is in that twelve seconds of space that can affect you. So you're going to be scanning ahead and behind you via your mirrors. Now when Mrs. Smith is sitting at that corner, looking like she MAY be turning left, but you're not sure, what are you going to do? Are you going to speed up, hoping to beat her to the intersection so she doesn't pull out in front of you? Are you going to come to a dead stop in your lane giving her the right of way? Or are you going to slow down, beep your horn, and cover your levers and brake pedal in case you have to make an emergency stop, evasive maneuvers or slow down?

You're going to slow down, make sure your high beam is on, beep your horn, cover both brake and clutch levers and the foot operated brake pedal and be prepared for whatever bone headed move she's going to make. If she doesn't then you're okay. If she does, and you're prepared, then you escape again, safely. Never stop dead in your lane, especially while your concentration is focused ahead of you. If you feel you have to stop because someone is going to jet out into your path of travel, then pull to the side. You do not want to be rear-ended by someone else not paying attention behind you.

Is all this starting to sound complicated? Well it really isn't. It's more of a routine than anything. So get yourself into the routine of wearing the riding gear all the time, of scanning the road twelve seconds around you at all times, and of being prepared for the worst, because it can and possibly will happen.

Recently, while I was attending the Americade rally in Lake George, NY, when on a test ride of a new ZX-10 Kawasaki, a mini-van drifted into my oncoming path (Meaning her left wheels crossed the yellow line, and part of this mini-van was actually in my lane.) Less than twenty seconds later, a left turning car jumped out in front of me as I came around a blind right hand turn. If I had been pushing this unfamiliar bike, I could have been in trouble, with either scenario, all in less than half a minute. Think about that. You must always ride like your life depends on it, because it literally does.

Okay, so now you're pulling into that donut shop to get your cup of coffee, and you roll the bike into a space. You plop down the kick stand, get off the bike and begin walking towards the door of the donut shop when you hear a sickening thud. You turn around, already knowing what happened before seeing it. Your baby is lying on its side. How did this happen? What did you do wrong? Actually a few things. When pulling into a parking space, always take into account the slope, or downhill angle of the ground. You want to park the bike with the nose facing away from the downhill slope of the ground. In other words, if the ground is sloping downwards towards the front of the space, park the rear of the bike towards that slope, or slant. Always park the nose uphill. Make sure you always leave the bike in first gear, not in neutral. If it's in neutral, it will roll off the kickstand. Make sure you always turn and lock the steering head. This will also stop the bike from rolling. Now go inside and enjoy that coffee and donut!

Chapter Four

So I've got you thinking about what can happen out there now, right? Good. You should be concerned. Because everything from parking lot drops to the uncaring driver pulling out in front of you, is only the start of what may happen out on the road. We're going to talk about more of these occurrences right now, and how you can be prepared for them.

An hour later you and Bernie are in a great riding area, and Bernie is really cooking. He's strafing apexes like he was Valentino Rossi. You see him ahead of you as he disappears around a bend, then you hear a sickening crunch, your stomach tightens as you round the bend, already slowing down because you were paying attention to what was going on ahead of you, and Bernie obviously was not.

You find Bernie lying on his back, bleeding and gasping for air, and his bike is destroyed. Looking around you see his tire tracks running through a pile of cow dung, and from there you can see where Bernie lost control, as his wheels slid out from under him in the slippery mess. Luckily you have your Cell phone and an ambulance is on the way.

But if Bernie had been wearing the proper protective gear, he would be in much better shape than he is now. He will require surgery and months of recuperation time to get back on his feet again.

So is this reason to give up motorcycling? That's a personal choice. To some, yes. To others, and some for the wrong reason (The same one Bernie had "It'll never happen to me.") the answer is a resounding "No."

What did Bernie do wrong? Let's start at the beginning. Bernie took it for granted that he'll always be okay and that his skill will save him from anything. In a better, more well prepared rider, who is honest with himself about his abilities, this accident would never have happened, because he A) would not have been going as fast as Bernie was. B) He would have been wearing head to toe riding gear, no matter what temperature it was, and C) He would have realized that anything can happen over that next section of roadway.

Always ride with your head, no matter what. Think before you go out there and become a blood splat on the pavement. Approach unknown areas with caution, not machismo. You could fly around a corner as a deer steps out of the woods right into your path, and this happens every day.

Time for another scenario. What happens when it's 80-90 degrees out, and you're out for a day ride in the country? Well the first thing that happens is that those squiggly lines in the tar, known as "Tar snakes" begin to soften up.

What do I mean by soften up? Well the sun bakes them, and like anything that gets heated, something happens to them. In this case, they become soft. The next time you get a hot day. Stop on the side of an empty road and put your foot on top of a tar snake, then move your foot around. The tar snake will move with you.

Now imagine you're rolling over that tar

snake, and you have to lean and turn as the road curves away ahead of you. One or both of your tires could momentarily seemingly slide away on you. Not a good thing, or a reassuring feeling. One that could seemingly cause panic and that would be all it would take to make you lose control, and end up in a ditch somewhere.

Another road hazard is the painted stripes on roadways, though these are a double hazard, as they can soften somewhat like tar snakes, though not to that degree and they also become VERY slippery when wet.

How do we as motorcyclists handle these hazards? Well in both cases above, we take them straight on and upright as much as possible. Try not to be leaned over in a turn when crossing either of these in inclement weather of any type. It's yet another situation that you have total control over, if you only think ahead.

So now you are riding along towards a meeting with some friends, and you're on a two lane highway doing at or around the speed limit. (65-75 MPH) You are in the middle lane of the highway, when you suddenly see the car next to you veering into your lane, right into you! What do you do?

You quickly look right and cut into that lane, but if that lane had traffic in it, you would have been in big trouble. How could you have avoided that situation? On a bike, you should always be in the far left lane of whatever road you're on, so you avoid the driver looking to go either left or right who is not paying attention to his driving. (There are many distractions car drivers generally fall into. Men shaving with electric razors while driving, Cell phones, kids crying the back seat, women applying makeup. The list goes on ad nauseam.) Avoid riding in the right or center lanes of any highway. The left is the safest. You only have one area to concentrate your attention on, that being to the right of you. Now if a car starts to come into your lane from the right without realizing you are there, you can either speed up safely, or drop back letting him in. Blow your horn; do not be afraid to use it. It's there for a reason. Now when you have the impatient driver behind you who wants to blister the speed limit, you can easily slip momentarily into the center lane and let him pass, then slide back into the left lane.

    Riding in the right lane opens a whole other set of problems. You have the entering and exiting drivers who either realize they are about to miss their exit, or those entering the highway, who will do anything to force their way onto the road. And what is the first thing a motorist says when they hit a motorcyclist? "I didn't see him." In these scenarios, it's something that is heard over and over. You have to protect yourself by riding pro-actively. That alone allows us to continue to enjoy this sport for years to come.

    Another situation that commonly happens is you approach a corner in a light rain that has just begun, and you suddenly end up on the ground. What happened? Well, in any rain, you should pull over somewhere and sit for about fifteen minutes, and let the ground get good and wet, washing away the covering of oil that coalesces there from repeated leaking cars. Also, it's not just oil that causes bikes and riders to crash. Anti-freeze is as slippery as ice! It's best to avoid anti-freeze at all costs. If you see any wet spots on a dry day, ride around them, especially if they are green or blue colored. Any time you suspect rain or get caught in a rainstorm, find shelter and pull over. I myself have pulled under the awning of hardware stores as well as simply stopping at a coffee shop where I sat inside and waited a storm out over a soda. I've also pulled under the shelter of an underpass and sat out serious Thunderstorms. If the rain continues for any amount of time, and you are local to home. Then grit your teeth and head out, making sure you are leaving double the amount of space between you and the vehicle in front of you. (If you normally leave two seconds, which should be your minimum, leave four, I know, easier said than done, especially in congested areas, but do what you can. After all, if you crash and end up injured the guy in the car who was complaining about you leaving so much space in front of yourself will still be home for dinner, and you won't!)

    When traveling, make sure you either have a rain suit that will fit over your riding gear with you, or buy a waterproof set of riding gear

Chapter Five

Speaking of rain riding... Riding in the rain requires a whole different set of gear. One that must be carried in addition to your everyday gear. Again, if you are local to home you can always bear ten to fifteen minutes worth of rain. But when you are traveling, rain gear is a must! It's something that every rider should have. Companies such as Tour master, Sterns, Motoport, First Gear and many more make rain suits that will fit right over your regular riding gear.

Of course you could also buy a waterproof riding suit, but the problem with that is that they are very hot, much more so than a suit that breathes. But these are your rain suit options.

Other gear to consider for a rainy day are things like waterproof gloves, or over mittens. Waterproof gloves are great, but there are very few that actually work. A company named "Olympia" makes one such pair, for example the Olympia "Monsoon" gloves. But they are difficult to get on and off at best. They do work though. Another option is a set of over mittens. These are waterproof nylon Mittens that go over your regular riding gloves, keeping your hands dry.

Now that we've taken care of your body and hands, what about your feet? There are many manufacturers that claim their boots are waterproof, but only a few actually are. Again, to me the best answer is a set of over boots, cousin of the over mitten! Tour master, Motoport, First Gear and may more make these, and they are all relatively inexpensive, usually under $30! More importantly, they actually do work. I ride with a pair of Alpinestar N1's, which are motorcycle boots that look and wear like sneakers. They are light enough for walking around in, and have armored protection for my ankles as well as double thick rubber for my toes. They are not waterproof though. Yet with a pair of boot gaiters on, they definitely are closer to it!

    I recently read an article concerning a motorcyclist who was struck by lightning while riding. He was killed instantly. Don't think it can't happen, because it already has. When it thunderstorms out, best to find shelter, and let it pass. Most thunderstorms pass in only a few minutes time.

    Another inclement condition to avoid is cold weather riding. And by cold I mean below forty degrees. Some will argue that you can successfully ride all year long with the proper gear on. This is a personal preference. I myself stop at forty degrees.

    Have you heard of "Hypothermia"? Hypothermia is the condition wherein the body loses heat faster than it can be produced by muscle contractions, shivering, or the metabolism. This condition usually occurs when the body is exposed to cold water, such as a cold, driven rain. But it can occur in simple cold weather as well. When riding in cold weather, always take into consideration the outside temperature and the speed you will be traveling. For instance, if it is forty degrees outside, and you are riding at seventy miles per hour, do you know what the air temperature will be? Ten degrees. That's right you'll be riding in ten degree cold, due to the speed you will be traveling. Dress appropriately when riding in cold weather and don't underestimate the effect cold will have on you. Hypothermia is not something to be trifled with; it can lead to unconsciousness and death if left untreated. This is VERY serious stuff.

There are ways to extend your riding season if you need to though. Electric vests and jackets are the best way. They plug into your bikes electrical system, draw very little power, but warm your upper body, and with the optional electric gloves several manufacturers make, your hands as well. The important thing they do is warm your core. Your core is your upper body, where all your organs reside. By keeping this area warm you can ride well into the twenty-degree range, if you so choose.

If you decide to go the traditional non-electric route for winter riding gear, you can always get a suit with an optional cold weather lining, as well as heavy winter gloves. Make sure you wear heavier, ski type socks as well. Most riding suits have linings that zip into and out of the pants. These are invaluable on a motorcycle in the cold weather.

Is your head cold? Then get yourself a Balaclava. Basically a thin, nylon, silk or cotton mask that has the face open below your lip and above your eyes. It makes you neck warm as well as your head inside the cold helmet on a winter day. You'll be surprised at how much better you feel when you are warm in the core and on your head. Did you know that you lose body heat out of the top of your head?

Another important piece of the puzzle for cold or rain weather riding is your tires. Now most people for some unknown reason ignore their tires. But tires are all that keep you in contact with the road. To do so, they have to be properly inflated, as well as in good riding condition. Yet most of the time people do not check their tires often enough. I constantly hear people complaining about their bikes not handling well any more, or how the bike no longer felt like it did when new. Yet if they took the time to inspect their tires once a week, they would see the gradual decrease of shape, and the "Squaring off" that occurs with all tires from every day use.

It also depends on your riding style and what area of the country you live in, as far as how much mileage you'll get out of a set of tires. I get anywhere from nine to twelve thousand miles out of a set on either of my bikes, yet I know others who live in hotter climates routinely get only a few thousand miles out of theirs.

If your tires are old (More than say, three years.) and have cracks appearing in them, it's time for a new set. If they are squared off (In other words, no longer have a rounded shape to the body of the tire.) And are down to the wear indicators (The bars that go across the tire every few inches and form flat lines when the rest of the tire is worn down to it.) Then it is time for a new set of tires. Motorcycle tires are nothing to be cheap about. That three to four inch contact patch is all that holds you to the road. Treat it like your life depends on it, because it does. ESPECIALLY in inclement weather.

Chapter Six

We've talked about bad weather and about riding gear, as well as a few of the things that can happen to you on any day. We also touched on tires at the end of the last chapter; we're going to talk more about them right now.

Okay, you know those two hula hoop looking things that go round and round on either end of your bike? They are called Tires. They are made of primarily rubber, along with aramid or steel fibers, and a lot of nylon, depending on what brand and type of tire you are using. What most riders forget to do, is to check the air pressure. Once again, I hear plenty of riders complaining about how their bikes ride and handle, but it is not the bikes fault in a lot of these occurrences, it is that the tires simply do not have enough air pressure in them. Use your manufacturers recommended air pressures, which can be found in your owner's manual. In a months' time a tire can drop several pounds. That is why it is a good habit to develop to check them once every week.

What kind of tires should you put on your bike? There are actually many different specialized types of tires. Some are more sport oriented called, amazingly enough, "Sport" tires. These tires are very "Soft", and wear quickly. Soft tires stick to the ground better than a harder tire, making your attachment to the pavement while riding almost glue-like. You slide less and have a surer grip. The downside is that they wear out faster. On a bike that you do long trips on, these are not the tire for you.

A "Sport touring" tire gives you the best of both worlds. They are far stickier then a touring tire, but also give more mileage then a sport tire. The down side to these is that they are normally harder than a sport tire, and while they grip excellently, they do not give the grip a pure sport tire does. They also tend to be affected more by colder temperatures. Their warm up time is somewhat longer than a softer tire, so you must ride slower, and safer longer.

Then there are full out touring tires for the big touring bikes like Goldwing's, Ventures, LT's and others which are not made at all for aggressive riding, rather they are made for simple touring and enjoying the road at a moderate pace, though I've seen Goldwing riders blister the speed limits on many occasions as well as any sport bike rider.

There are also varying qualities of tire. Different manufacturers usually mean different quality standards. Bridgestone, Michelin, Dunlop, Pirelli, Metzler and Avon are the top manufacturers right now. There are economy tires out there by various other manufacturers that do nothing but offer a less expensive alternative to the higher priced brands. This is not necessarily a bad thing, but just know what you are buying. You do get what you pay for, and it is always good to keep that in mind when researching items like tires, which are all that stand between you and the road.

Earlier I touched on squaring off. This is what happens when your tire wears and develops a flat spot. You can recognize this by the fact that it looks like those stupid haircuts from the early '90s. When you see flat spots developing, check your wear indicators. If the tire is not flush with them yet then just be aware that you will soon need a new set of contact patches.

Now I just used a term, "Contact Patch" and you are wondering just what a contact patch is? A contact patch is the point of contact where your tire touches the road. A car has four contact patches, and every one is at least two to four times a motorcycles contact patch width. We only have two tires, so our tires have to be stickier. Motorcycle tires also tend to wear much faster than car tires because of all this sticking around.

Now these are things we do not normally think about, but the truth is, when things go wrong, they affect us quickly, and decidedly painfully. So what does this mean to you? It means check your tires for air pressure, tread depth and visibly for cracking on a weekly basis. When you see cracking on a tire, it means that the tire has become "Dry Rotted". I know what you're thinking, "This guy is hitting us with yet another term I've never heard before." Well get used to it tough guy, there are plenty more coming.

Dry rotting is what a tire does when it gets old. The rubber separates, and begins to crack and split. These cracks can actually lead to blowouts, and on a motorcycle, that is far more dangerous than in a car, and look how bad those are!

So do yourself a huge favor and take care of your bike's tires. If they are more than a few years old, replace them, even if they look good. When the rubber hardens from age, you lose traction ability. When you put a new set of tires on, you'll be pleasantly surprised how much better the bike will feel all around, and by keeping up with your tire pressures, you'll not only increase your safety factor, you'll also increase the bikes efficiency.

Did that last sentence give you pause? Good it was meant to. When tires get low on air pressure, they tend to not only get squirrelly on the road, they use more gas. You can also suffer a blowout when riding with low air pressure. That would ruin your day for sure! They create more "Rolling resistance" Now you might think "Well it is making the bike stick to the road better, how can that be a bad thing? It is because the tire heats up quicker and expands more. It does not roll as easily, and now it will have a tendency to slide a bit under you. All bad things. So do the correct thing and treat your tires right!

Chapter Seven

If these chapters had names this one would be called "The psychology of motorcycling, or why do you want to do it?"

Motorcycling is a sport that means so much too so many people. You have to ask yourself what you want to get out of it. If you want to annoy your neighbors with the sound of straight pipes on a Sunday morning (This is no joke, I actually had someone say that to me and tell me that was the only reason they wanted to get a bike.), or you want to showboat on a sport bike doing wheelies and stoppies, then do us all a favor and take up golf.

Motorcycling is something that will give you back whatever you give into it tenfold. You will suddenly see the world through different eyes. You will see things and smell scents you can never encounter while locked up in a car. The roads have a rhythm to them that no car will ever let you experience first-hand. If this is why you want to motorcycle, then you got it right the first time.

To ride a motorcycle is not about drawing attention to yourself and telling the world "I'm cool." It's about enjoying a very personal ride along roads that you would not normally pay any attention to otherwise. Motorcycling is fun, it's habit forming and it's healthy. In both mind and body, motorcycling is good for you. Now I'm not going to tell you to buy a motorcycle and forget the gym membership, but I will tell you certain muscles in your body will strengthen over time spent riding. Mostly stomach and leg muscles will feel the effects of a summer spent riding.

Mentally, motorcycling can be the best relaxant around. You can enjoy the trees above you, the heat of the sun on your back, the fresh aroma of recently cut grass, and so much more. Motorcycling always puts you in a better frame of mind.

Ask yourself why do you really want to do this? If it's for any of the good reasons given above, then go sit on a few bikes in a dealership nearby. Introduce yourself to the salesman, and strike up a friendly conversation. Become acquainted with those in your area that you will be dealing with. Find out first-hand what shops and dealers you should deal with and who you should stay away from. Connect with a local riding group, either via Internet, or through mutual friends. This is the best way to learn about dealers and shops in your area.

Work on becoming an ambassador of the sport of motorcycling. To do this you have to generate the proper image. You have to wear the right gear, you have to be available to answer people's questions about your bike, and you have to make those same people feel at ease around you. By becoming a good image of a motorcyclist, we all benefit in the long run.

    Motorcycling has had a black eye since the late 1940's, which began with the Hollister, Ca. incident, which was immortalized in Marlon Brando's "The wild one." Only in the past ten to fifteen years has motorcycling begun to be more readily accepted as a mainstream sport and activity.
    In the early 1960's, the Honda Corporation created an advertising campaign that shook the motorcycle world. "You meet the nicest people on a Honda." Eight little words that suddenly began to change the motorcycling world. It was now suddenly almost acceptable to ride a motorcycle because of Mr. Honda's slogan. The general public began to see riders not as the hooligans they were once thought to be. Instead, they were now seen as people almost like themselves. It took many years after that, and we still fight this battle even today, but Honda's slogan began great strides for motorcyclists around the world.
    But there were other obstacles to motorcyclists being generally accepted as well. One was the misconception here in the United States that motorcycles were only pleasure vehicles. Over the Atlantic, in Great Britain and Europe, mostly due to higher gas prices, motorcycles are used as a daily means of travel, not just as pleasure vehicles.
    Which brings us back to the question "Why do you want to ride a motorcycle?" If you are in it

for the thrill of doing something different and discovering new things, then bravo! You got it right. Motorcycling opens up a plethora of new experiences for those who get involved in it for the correct reasons.

For those that are looking to be "cool" and are assuming that a motorcycle is the only way for that to happen, you should look elsewhere. Being a motorcyclist is actually in essence, making a commitment to learn something completely new, something you can learn from every day you're out there. It's not easy, but it is fun, and can be extremely rewarding. But that all depends on the individuals commitment. If you take it as a weekend only thing that you are doing for the ten-mile roundtrip to and from the local bike hang out, then you are doing it for the wrong reasons.

Remember, just by deciding to become a motorcyclist, you are already doing something that others will be in awe of, and will want to emulate. By presenting the correct image, you help out others as well as yourself. Think of Mr. Honda's slogan "You meet the nicest people on a Honda." and simply modify it a little to "You meet the nicest people on a motorcycle." And suddenly our whole preconceived image changes. There truly are a lot of nice people on motorcycles, when you become a motorcyclist you'll discover a group that goes out of its way for each other, and generally is a lot of fun to be around.

Chapter Eight

      Have you ever heard it been said that motorcyclists are their own worst enemies? No? Then what about bikers? Are they their own worst enemies? Truthfully, as long as people continue to do stupid, "look at me" stunts and make their motorcycles as loud as they can possibly be, people will be looking at every motorcycle as a threat to both their hearing and their physical well-being.

      Think I'm wrong? All over the country there are condominium complexes, as well as private neighborhoods with "No motorcycle" signs on their entrances, and there are more added almost weekly.

      Why you may ask? The answer is simple. Most people who ride motorcycles believe it is their God given right to ride and to do whatever they see fit, because they believe they are different. They are dead wrong. It is a privilege to ride, not a right.

      When you see that idiot kid doing a wheelie down the highway, the only ones cheering him on are either other idiot kids riding with him, or little children in the back of their parents cars that know no better, and are excited to see such an exciting looking stunt. Meanwhile their parents are shaking their heads at the stupidity and the dangerous actions of this squid, who if he should lose control and fall over, he can easily fall onto a car, injuring its passengers, or simply injure himself grievously, tying up traffic for some untold time.

      Do you know what "Squid" means? It's a

derogatory term that is hoisted upon riders who showboat and ride their motorcycles like fools, because chances are they are not wearing any riding gear, and when they fall, or "Go down" they'll leave a bloody stain on the pavement like a squid would when it shoots ink out. As well as their limbs being splayed all over the place in an awkward manner.

    Sounds gross doesn't it? It looks worse. Kids, especially new riders, or those with more guts than common sense and those that just want the world to look at them in some sort of glowing spotlight tend to do stunts and high speed antics all over the public roadways. If not actually "Stunting" they will ride at excessive speeds and weave in and out of traffic, usually for no other reason than to say, and to show the world that they could.

    Some do this on bikes as diverse as sport touring rigs, or full blown touring bikes, whose riders swear they are the best out there, and just want to prove it to their fellow riders.

    Others do it for personal merit, just to prove to themselves they've got the right stuff, and are the fastest of the fast.

    They are wrong, each and every one of them. When I see a rider rolling by on one wheel, I get annoyed almost instantly. It's not exciting or impressive. It's another blemish we don't need. It's another kid on a street corner motioning to me to do a wheelie, which has become so prevalent this past year as to be a daily occurrence. This stuff never happened in years past. Only in recent years, with the advent of the stunter crowd have riders been questioned by almost every kid out there to do a wheelie at every possible chance.

This is not a good thing. It brings a bad aspect of our sport into the spotlight. There are reports on nightly newscasts all over the country about riders exceeding speeds of 150 mph, and of riders leaving Police in the dust when they turn their lights on to give chase for some reckless act the motorcyclist did.

How long will actions like this go unpunished? We are not different than those around us, we have to obey the same laws as the drivers in their cars. If a posted speed limit is 35 mph, don't think it's okay for you to do 70 mph through that same section of road, just because you can. There are no separate laws for motorcycles. But if these riders continue to act this way, there soon will be, and they will not be in the way most motorcyclists believe they would like.

Motorcycles will not only be banned from certain communities, they will be banned from entire towns and from sections of roadway that have had a large share of motorcycle related accidents. Don't think it can't happen. All it takes is one elected official whose constituents have had enough of seeing hooliganism resulting in injuries or death to start trying to get bills pushed through that will hamper or limit motorcycles from certain thoroughfares, and that will be the beginning of more hard times for us all.

I have heard many tales of riders who were simply riding along minding their own business, who are pulled over by a Police officer and have their motorcycles given a thorough going over as well as having been made to answer fifty questions, before being given the go ahead to leave.

This becomes more and more common place every day.

So what other factors affect us detrimentally besides the "Biker Boyz" wannabe's out there? The loud pipe crowd is always a thorn in the side of motorcycling. Loud pipes risk rights, they do not save lives as the AMA puts it.

What's the AMA? Well it's NOT the American Medical Association. What it is, is the "American Motorcyclist Association". The AMA is large group of motorcyclists who fight for the rights of other motorcyclists across the country on various issues. These include land use for off road (dirt bike) riders, the aforementioned inaccessibility of certain areas to motorcyclists, and various other motorcycle related issues, including fighting for the families of motorcyclists killed by careless drivers who otherwise would get away free and clear without any sort of punishment. You can check out the American Motorcyclist Association on the World Wide Web at www.amadirectlink.org

Getting back to the loud pipes issue, loud pipes do nothing for safety. They merely make a motorcycle loud. As I've said elsewhere in this book, they are for the "Look at me" personality who simply craves attention. While not all loud pipes are bad, straight pipes are by far the worst of the lot and are in total disregard for everyone around them. A throaty, rumbling pipe that is simply of good tone and resonance is sometimes pleasing to hear. But a scratchy, broken up sounding, completely open pipe

(Meaning no baffling material inside the pipe to quiet it at all.) is obnoxious and gives the sport as a whole a continued bloody nose.

Do you think this stuff doesn't matter and that no one can bother you if you ride with open pipes? Think again. Many communities have instigated a Police watch where they check every motorcycle coming through with a decibel meter to see if it meets federal noise regulations. If the motorcycle fails the test, the rider gets a costly ticket. What a nice way to start your day, right?

But this is the cost of things we bring about ourselves. This is the reason I say we are our own worst enemies.

Every time a motorcycle goes by either doing an excessive amount of speed (Like over a hundred miles per hour as an example.) on a public road, in front of an audience of unwilling onlookers. Wheelies and stoppies (Front wheel lofted in the air, or rear wheel upon a very hard stop.) Burnout's, (Applying large amounts of throttle and locking the front brake until the rear tire burns rubber spinning, and creates large clouds of smoke.) and assorted other stupidity are all bad marks against us as a whole. No matter what you are doing, when you are trolling along, riding slightly above the surrounding traffics speed, minding your own business, we all run the risk of being lumped together as another "dangerous outlaw biker" riding his "murdercycle" because of those around us who continue to annoy and aggravate a society that does not understand, or see the need to understand and enjoy our sport.

Why should they? We are a small percentage

of the population. In fact, there are to this day, still a significant number of riders who refuse to get licensed. This is yet another bad stigma that we as a group do not need. The facts do not lie, motorcyclists can be looked at in a negative light, and it is our own fault. For this and many more reasons, we are our own worst enemies. For years responsible motorcyclists have had to fight the outlaw image, no matter what they ride.

So how do we combat the bad image that goes along with our sport to some degree? By projecting an image of responsibility and just not riding foolishly. Everything we do on the road in front of others bears down on us all. We have to remain a courteous group to others, waving when people let us into a lane, talking to others who ask us about our motorcycles, and generally letting people who have no clue about motorcycling know that we're just like them. In a nutshell, we make people realize what great people we are by dispelling the bad guy image.

Now many of you may want nothing to do with this, and that's okay. Just go out and ride your motorcycles, but try not to add to the bad stigma that's already there.

Chapter Nine

The time has come for you to take your first real ride. You've already checked your bike out thoroughly, you know the tire pressure is good and that the bike is in good, safe riding condition. Now you just have to make sure you are.

You tuck your bootlaces into the boots themselves (If they have laces) you don't want those flopping around, especially on a chain driven bike. Next you zip up your jacket and tighten your gloves around your wrists. You cinch up your chinstrap and lower your helmet face shield in place. You set the choke and pull in the clutch lever and the front brake lever and hit the start button. Let the bike warm up a minute or two, your bike will love you for this! Next, you ease out of your driveway, checking side to side repeatedly. You never know when a stray child will appear out of nowhere, as well as a stray car. Roll out onto your road and start moving. Now remember in your neighborhood, or wherever you live, you're going to be lackadaisical because you think you know everything that can happen to you there. You've lived there a good, long time, and know the road as well as what you think to expect.

But here is where you can get hurt just as easily if not more so than anywhere else! It's because of that very same lackadaisical attitude that comes with familiarity. Think when you ride! ALWAYS have thoughts running through your mind of what can happen to you if a dog should suddenly jump a fence right into your path. A friend had this very thing happen to him and he ended up in the hospital for weeks, and has to live with the memory of splitting the dog in two for the rest of his life. Not to mention, his bike being a total loss. Always be thinking. Always be scanning ahead.

Your first stop will be a gas station, where you'll fill your tank. You stop at the pump. What's the first thing you should do? Put the kickstand down. Now with the kickstand down upright the bike to fill the tank, but have the kickstand down just in case you let it go for some reason. (Always fill the bikes tank while it is perfectly upright, you'll get the most gas possible in the tank, as opposed to losing out on some capacity by leaving it leaned over.) Stay seated, balance the bike with your body and legs and fill the tank to the limit described in your owners' manual.

Okay, you have gas, you have a destination (beyond your local coffee & donut shop) and you are ready to roll. Pull out to the driveway edge of the gas station and make sure you can see any traffic that might impede your progress, then roll out and take off at a moderate pace, not blazing like a skyrocket.

Suddenly you hear a horn blowing and see a car careening towards you, with the driver waving his fist at you. You escape unscathed, but it could have been much worse! What happened? What went wrong? The car driver never saw you. It could have been anything attributing to it. Glare, loss of concentration on his part, someone talking to him. What could you have done to avoid this?

One of the most important things a rider can do is to use his high beam in the daytime, and not the low beam. You become so much more visible to oncoming cars. That alone can be a lifesaver. The common complaint from drivers who have hit motorcycles is that they did not see the motorcycle. Make yourself visible at all times!

You have to also be constantly aware of what's going on around you at all times. No daydreaming. So practice in your spare time off the bike looking around you and identifying everything that can affect you. Look for sand in corners and on road shoulders. Learn to identify gravel as well. These things cannot become your attention points though. You have to basically be aware of them peripherally and then move on to the next possible problem.

What is the next possible problem you ask? There is an almost infinite amount, but your brain has to work like a virus scan program does on your computer, always on, always working, and in the background. You have to process every possible threat to yourself and leave enough escape room to have an out at all times. The first thing this means is no excessive speed in areas you are not familiar with. So don't go buzzing that side street at twice the legal speed limit and expect nothing to happen. We are made aware of horror stories every day about bike-car collisions in just such a setting. You have to pad your safety zone in your favor. Remember, anything can happen. A ball could suddenly appear in front of you, or an animal, or worse yet, a child chasing that ball or animal. Ride responsibly. Always be thinking.

    What else is going on around you right now? Does the car to your right even know you are there? Make sure that they do. How you ask? Simply, pull up out of their blind spot. Don't put yourself behind, or beside the driver's head, if possible. Always ride slightly faster than traffic when you can. Make yourself visible. Loud pipes DO NOT save lives. They make noise. The only thing that will save your life is to be thinking clearly and ahead of everyone around you. Always be in a lane position where you are visible and able to move over to one side or the other. In other words, be in the center of the lane. There are exceptions to this rule. One is on group rides, you have to ride in staggered position (We will touch on this later on in the group riding chapter) the other is during a rain that has just started. At that occurrence, you will put your bike into a cars tire tracks, in either the left or right track for the first ten to fifteen minutes of any rainstorm. Preferably, as I said before, you will sit it out for the first few minutes of a storm to let the oils accumulated by cars passing by to run off, because during the first few minutes of any rainstorm or shower the pavement is the slickest it can be. If you cannot get out of the rain, even for a few minutes, then plant your bike into a tire track and allow twice your normal road distance. You normally allow two seconds between you and the vehicle in front of you? Now allow four.

But how do you account for time? Very easily, Grasshopper...

Chapter Ten

When learning about motorcycling, you will come upon many sources of information. Some will be Internet based, most will be in the form of books, such as this one, and magazines. You will also find that some sources contradict others, as with all things in life. You must decide what makes the most sense for you. Also, take into consideration that some of the authors you will be reading in the coming months and years are racers, and while much of what they say is pertinent to everyday street use, some of it will not be.

Such as what I am about to impart to you, dear reader. How do you tell what distance you should be from the vehicle in front of you? You count the seconds. Pick a spot on the ground, be it a section of dotted line, or a signpost, or any marking you feel comfortable with. Wait until the rear tire of the vehicle in front of you passes over that mark and begin counting "One thousand one, one thousand two." That accounts for two seconds of distance between you and the vehicle in front of you. That is the MINIMUM distance you want between you and another vehicle. You would be better served to stretch that to three to four seconds, though modern day traffic does not allow that in most instances.

This technique takes little effort, and after conscientiously doing this for a short time, you will find yourself counting off automatically on rides. This distance equals a buffer or safety zone for you in case of a panic situation ahead of you.

Now what about the zone behind you? There

will be times when you notice a car following much too closely, and you will recognize this automatically, because his or her distance behind you will be less than you would find yourself following when doing the "Count".

In these instances, it is best to simply either momentarily move to another lane, out of the trailing vehicles path, or to, as a first attempt, tap your brake pedal a few times to gather that drivers attention. If after a few attempts at that, they are still following too closely, then immediately move out of their path of travel to another lane, or if on a one lane road, pull over out of their way at your earliest convenience.

Getting out of their way is really the best thing to do, because even if they do "Wake up" and realize they were following you too closely, they are apt to do it again when their attention is once again diverted from their driving. Best to get out of their way at the beginning, before a problem has a chance to occur.

When a fellow rider is following too closely, wave your left hand at him in a gesture of "get back". If he does not back off, assuming he is a friend and you are riding with him, pull over and tell him he is riding to closely to you and you are uncomfortable with it. He should either back off at least two seconds from your bike, or pass you, but inform him in either case that he is being unsafe. If he doesn't like it, well that's just too bad. Your safety is paramount, not his ego.

We're going to touch on group riding in a whole chapter later on, but I will say a little bit about it right here. First and foremost, be organized. If someone is riding within the group and is in your opinion a "hot dog" feel free to tell him or her. To many times people hold their tongues only to see an accident later on that day involving this same person. The real tragedy of it becomes clear when someone else is taken down due to this person's foolishness.

A person who is detrimental to a groups ride is usually someone who has a large ego, and is new to the group of riding buddies. Instead of simply finding his spot in the group, he will try to force his way in and show his "Superior" riding skills. He will ride stupidly, sometimes on shoulders around other riders, he will be obnoxious, and he will perform plenty of attention getting antics. When you see these qualities, ask this person to leave. No good can come of it. You should also have the group ask him to go as a whole.

One of the main reasons riders in group situations crash is because they lose their focus. They are either concerned with someone else on the ride they are watching (A girlfriend, a relative, etc.) or they are daydreaming about what a nice day it is or some other thing that takes their attention away from where it should be, which is on their riding.

Also, understand that group riding means more than one bike. It does not necessarily mean three to four plus motorcycles.

Other obstacles in the road can ruin your day whether solo or in a group. Always be aware of where you are and what can happen at any time. I mentioned earlier that a deer could pop out of nowhere at any time. This is an all too common occurrence. There are many others to be aware of.

So eyes front and scanning as well as hitting the mirrors to make sure you are not about to be run over. Make sure you identify possible threats like pieces of wood, small animals like squirrels and chipmunks at the roadside. Be on the lookout for gravel in corners (very dangerous!) as well as items dropping off of trucks. Many times you will see trucks loaded to overflowing with debris. When you do, stay back! Either that or make a controlled pass and get away from that vehicle. If their truck is loaded that badly, you run a good chance of getting beaned by something dropping off of it. If you HAVE to run over a board or something that just fell off a truck, then do so while completely upright, not while leaned over. Loose grip on the bars, your weight on the foot pegs, and continue rolling right over whatever it is. It's better not to stiffen up which would make you take the impact as a jarring shock, as opposed to a much lesser, softer impedance to your day.

One of the most dangerous obstacles facing a motorcyclist comes when riding the highway. You will find wide, long strips of rubber on shoulders all over America's interstate system. These are pieces of truck-recapped tires, or recaps as they are more commonly referred to, and they are very, very dangerous, even deadly to a motorcyclist. Stay away from tractor-trailers. If one of those recaps blows off the rim and hits you, you'll be finished before you even realize it! I can't say enough how dangerous those recaps are.

There are other dangers on the highways as

well. The highways are places where you won't find Deer or Moose for the most part (There are exceptions to every rule!) but you will find the aforementioned recaps as well as pieces of overhead signs that have fallen. (One of these destroyed a motor on a friend's bike on a season beginning ride. So watch out, this stuff DOES indeed happen.) Road hazard signs that have blown into the road, becoming a hazard themselves. Areas of construction must be watched, as pavement changes to sometimes no pavement at all complicate matters. Road spills are another such hazard that could impede the motorcyclist for more than the car driver. A slippery substance that has spilled out of a truck will slow a car down for the most part, but a motorcycle it will put down! Adjust your speed accordingly.

If by chance you come upon a road spill of some kind, and there is no way to avoid it, ride through it perfectly upright, and coasting. I would even think pulling the clutch in would be a good idea, so there is no engine drag being applied to your rear wheel. Once clear of it, resume your riding, but remember to take it easy, or even to pull over and look at your tires to see what they look like, if any of this substance is covering your tires, making them lose adhesion. Ride conservatively until you are satisfied that whatever substance this is has worn off your tires.

Always be prepared to cover your brakes and use them at a half seconds notice, because if you get that much time in an emergency situation, consider yourself lucky!

One other item you should periodically

inspect are your tires. Look for dry rot of course, but also look for any shiny metallic objects protruding from the treads. It could be a nail or a screw. Check these as many times as you can remember, because it would be less than fun to have to deal with a flat tire while alone in a sparsely populated area.

Chapter Eleven

I mentioned brakes at the end of the last chapter, and that's what we're going to talk about in this one. There is a lot to discuss when talking brakes, beyond popular belief.

For instance, one of the oldest arguments in motorcycling is whether you should use all four fingers on the front brake lever, or just two? Some say that too many fingers will result in locked up front brakes and a possible low side. I say no, because you should be practicing your braking in a dry, sand and debris free environment every so often. You have to take your bike and go to a parking lot that has "clean" pavement. Once there, practice panic stops. The point here is to learn the limits of your tires and brakes adhesion, not to crash or dump your bike. You have to familiarize yourself with how your bike stops under hard braking. Now don't go and just grip the lever for all it's worth. You have to learn to modulate your brake lever and pedal. Doing this in an area that is traffic free is the right way to learn your limits, after all you don't want to be doing any emergency braking on a crowded road, and end up either lying on your back, or simply scared witless by an unexpected occurrence.

Learn how your bike feels under hard braking. Then learn how it feels under steady modulation of the lever and the pedal, so you won't have any surprises when you least need them. Practice your panic stops. Set up cones and practice stopping distances to the cones.

First try stopping with front brake alone, then

return and do the exercise with only rear brake. Now, finally do the exercise one more time with both brakes. You'll see your stopping distances are greatly reduced. Don't be afraid of your rear brakes, they contain 25% of your stopping power. Consequently, the front brakes are MUCH more powerful. It is easy to panic and (especially with today extremely powerful sport bike brakes.) to lock the front wheel at one time or another.

You should never do this. It could result in the front end tucking beneath you, causing an accident, or the bike doing what is commonly referred to a "stoppie" or an "endo". What these are, is when the front tire locks so abruptly that the rear wheel flies off the ground.

When the rear wheel locks you can also lose control and end up doing what is called "High siding" the bike. What this means, is that the bike will begin to slide as if it were doing a low side crash, but if you release the rear pedal out of panic, the rear tire suddenly grabs traction again, and the motorcycle snaps up and over to the opposite side, smashing both you and the motorcycle to the ground. This is the worst kind of crash for a motorcyclist, short of a multi vehicle accident. In single vehicle collisions, this can be the most life threatening.

How do you avoid this? When coming to a stop, if you begin to feel the rear end locking up and sliding, keep the rear tire locked until the bike has stopped. Now there are exceptions to the rule. If you feel the bike just beginning to slide sideways, and not get too far out of control, then you can release the rear brake and re-apply it. BUT, only if the speed is low and you are not already sliding to the side. Anything other than what I just described will amount to a possible high side.

When riding, you should never apply brakes in a turn. This is dangerous and will result in accidents. All your braking should be done before the turn. Once you are in the turn you should be applying a minimal amount of throttle to make the rear end of the bike squat down, and grab traction.

Never grab a handful of brake during a turn, you will lose control and crash the bike.

To accomplish a smooth sweeping turn, sight through the turn to the far end of it, or as far as you can see. Brake before you get into the turn, scrubbing off as much speed as is necessary for you. Forget about the guy behind you. If he wants to ride faster than you are willing to ride; he can pass you on the next straight, after you wave him by.

When you have sufficiently lowered your speed to a comfortable level, roll on the throttle slightly, just enough to make the motorcycle squat down, and roll through the turn. You DO NOT have to roar through turns with the throttle wide open. Yes, that can be great fun, but it to can be dangerous. A little sand or gravel in those corners would mean an end to your fun for at least that day and perhaps a lot longer!

Always sight through turns as far as the eye can see, and never apply your brakes while leaned over. To do so is just asking for an accident.

Panic can make you grab your brake lever in a death grip! Never succumb to that. Continue to look to the end of the corner you're in and just lean the bike further over. Chances are you'll have plenty of clearance left to complete your turn. If not, you are riding too fast for the street.

Another question some riders have concerning braking is how many fingers should they use? Some prefer two fingers, others say to use all four. I say use all four, all the time, and always be prepared to use your brakes, covering the lever when you feel unsafe about a situation. Always be prepared to grab the brake lever and apply an amount of stopping power that will take you out of a situation developing in front of you. It's best to hold your handlebar ends in a loose grip, applying too much pressure will hurt your hands, eventually resulting in carpal tunnel. This also allows you to quickly move your hands to the levers and grab both to slow down quickly.

Notice I said "both"? Yes, you read that correctly. When braking, grab both levers. The clutch and the brake simultaneously. Make the bike stop faster. By not engaging your clutch, you will still be adding power to the rear wheel, and the bike will take longer to stop. By making the bike freewheeling (Engaging the clutch) the bike now stops much easier, and in far less distance. This is another exercise you can try in your deserted parking lot. Stop first with only engaging your clutch at the end of your stop. Then do it again and engage the clutch simultaneously with both brakes. You'll see a huge difference in stopping power, and you won't feel the characteristic drag of the motor slowing you down upon stopping.

There is also a technique used by racers and

track guys called "Trail braking" that involves dragging the rear brake while going through corners and sweepers, but it should NOT be used on the road. It could very easily be a cause of the rear wheel locking and sliding you off the road or high siding. So stay away from trail braking, but at least be aware of what it is.

Do you know what both "high siding" and "low siding" are? If not, we'll go over what they both are here. Low siding is when the bike slides out from under you to one side or the other, and you just flop on the ground and the bike slides away. A crash, but in most cases one, if wearing the proper gear, you can walk away from usually.

A high side is a different animal altogether. A high side is a violent slam to the pavement, caused by the motorcycle first going to one side in a loss of traction, then the tires finding their grip and the motorcycle righting itself violently, slamming over to the other side.

This usually results in serious injury, as I alluded to earlier. Avoid causing yourself a high side. They can be deadly and at the very least very painful. Remember to never lock your rear brake while in a turn! Practice leaning over further then you need to, just to know what it feels like. Again, setting up cones in a parking lot can go far towards your becoming a better rider. Use them as points to stop at, points to turn at, points to begin a turn at, and points to end turns at, as well as points to begin braking at.

Practice makes perfect. It's not just a silly old saying your grandmother used to repeat. Do you know it take the human brain something like one hundred and thirty repetitions of something to be permanently remembered in most cases? Start doing exercises for your riding. Practice, practice, practice!

Learn what your brakes feel like under a straight-line panic stop. Learn what they feel like when just easing into them. Most importantly, get into the habit of stopping with both front and rear brakes all the time. Remember to use the clutch at every stop, so it all becomes a habit you no longer even have to think about.

What do you do when your brakes are worn down? You have to replace them with something of at least equal performance. There are many brake manufacturers out there, Do some local research and find out what brands the people with your bike are happy with. It will vary between bikes. There are also some performance upgrades you can do to your brakes like braided steel brake lines for instance. They do not flex and expand like rubber does and you end up with MUCH more stopping power. There are different rotors you can try also. Though the simplest increase in braking power would come from installing a set of sintered brake pads instead of the organic or Kevlar ones that come with your bike.

The downside of sintered pads is that there is a chance of rotors warping from them or wearing down quicker. But you will find the stopping power greatly enhanced.

One of the best things you can do for your brakes is to bleed them once per year, and refill with new, fresh brake fluid. You'll keep your stopping power high and your pedal and lever feel stiff. The bike will stop better, and you'll maintain a high level of safety. A well-maintained bike is the first part of the braking equation. A well maintained you is the most important part!

Once a year, go over your brake lines and check for dry rot and general wear and tear. You definitely do not want any surprises with your brakes. When your brake lines exhibit any type of damage or wear, including wetness around fittings, immediately replace them. Damaged brake lines will end your riding season very quickly!

When changing brake lines or bleeding brakes, make sure to cover your tank with a few old towels to absorb any brake fluid that might spill. The old types of brake fluid would eat away paint very quickly. DOT 4 (Which is in most bikes these days.) doesn't seem to have that problem. Don't ask me how I know... But still, better to be safe than sorry! Always use a brand new container of brake fluid when bleeding brakes. Dispose of the unused stuff when finished.

Chapter Twelve

So now you know how to properly apply your brakes and how to practice that application to make yourself a better stopper. But how do you turn the motorcycle? Ah good question! Have you ever heard of "Counter steering"? Most beginning motorcyclists haven't. Don't feel bad if you're not any different. What is counter steering? It's a technique that every motorcyclist uses whether they realize it or not. Anywhere over somewhere around twenty MPH, you have to push your handlebar in the opposite direction you want it to go to accomplish a turn. I know, it sounds all wrong, but it's not. You want to go right; you push on the right bar. You want to go left; you have to push on the left bar. Crazy, right? No, it's actually not. All this has to do with the way a two-wheeled vehicle is set up, it's the way a motorcycle leans into a turn, and the way your weight is distributed over the motorcycle's body. Want to go right? Push right. Want to go left? Push left. This takes place like I said, anywhere over say, twenty-MPH or so. Anything under that, and you can turn the bike like you would normally think it should be done. You can even practice this technique on your bicycle. It's something you've been doing your whole life, whether or not you realize it.

In any case, counter steering is something you have to realize you are doing and how to control it. You cannot turn a bike any other way. There have been arguments about weighting the bike one way or another, and that counter steering is not an issue, but these arguments are always proven wrong.

Weighting the side of the bike you are turning into is something that should be done in conjunction with counter steering. What do I mean? Real simple. Lean INTO a turn, not away from it. While you are pushing your bar away from you, lean in that same direction. Many people lean away from their bars when pushing to counter steer. This straightens the bike up, and can be used when doing the around twenty MPH rule I mentioned earlier. If you lean away from the direction you are turning in, your bike will stand up, and you will lose lean angle. When you lean into a turn with the bike, you will increase lean angle and the bike will go deeper into the turn, enabling you to turn faster.

Another technique used in turning a motorcycle (Especially a sport or standard style bike) is to place the ball of your foot on the foot peg and step down as you turn, this of course being the same side of the bike you are turning into. This places your weight more directly on the correct side of the bike for the turn; it enables you to lean into a turn better, and pushes your bike towards the edges of its tires. You DO NOT want to overdo this. I've never seen, or heard of anyone crashing while attempting this technique, but anything is possible. I doubt very much you'll ever push your bike beyond its tire's traction limits on the sidewalls. But best to try this a little bit at a time to get a feel for it.   Also, try to make the foot placement a habit so that you are doing it at every turn instinctively.

All of these techniques should eventually become something you no longer even think about, and just naturally do.

I mentioned in an earlier chapter looking through a turn. I'm going to refresh your memory here and then talk about it some more.

When you are entering a turn, your eyes should be at the far end of the turn. Not directly in front of you, not staring at the rear tire of the bike in front of you, not staring at the back of that riders head, not staring at the rider in front of him, but as far ahead as you can see through that turn. You will see the motorcycles ahead of you peripherally, and if you are following our two-second rule, you'll have plenty of stopping time available if something should go amiss.

Also, you will have slowed substantially before entering the turn, especially a blind one. Remember to always be slightly on the throttle when rolling through a turn, this plants the rear end of the bike firmly into the turn, and transfers weight where it should be, on the drive (rear) wheel.

When you look through a turn, keep your eyes focused on the end of the turn, or at least as far as you can see towards that end. The motorcycle will go where your eyes point it, not where you want it too automatically. This is a hand-eye coordination thing that we do without realizing it.

I always keep my speed down when in a turn until I can see the exit of the turn, then I accelerate through it, all the while keeping slightly on the gas to squat the rear tire down.

The unexpected can happen in a turn as well. You never know when a board that has fallen off of a truck will suddenly appear in your path! Never mind the ever-present threat of wildlife! Now it is always easier to say something then to do it, but if you happen to have this occurrence, or something even vaguely similar, the best thing to do is to stand the bike up if possible, roll over the offending object, brake if need be while upright, then to get back into your turn immediately. Never stab at your brake lever in panic. It's best to train yourself to have a cool head in a situation like this, and to act accordingly. We sometimes do things in a reflexive nature, and this is the action that will most likely get us into trouble on the road.

When navigating several switchback type turns one after another, you will first weight the peg to the side you are turning, while you are simultaneously pushing on the same side bar, and positioning your body towards that side of the bike, leaning into the turn. Then you will immediately repeat the maneuver on the other side of the bike. You may have to do this several times, depending on the road you are riding on.

This brings us to the next point. Some areas of the country have much better riding roads than others. Where I live, the roads are mostly straight, with many lights and stop signs. To get to good, curvy roads, I have to travel at least an hour and a half. So the roads you become used to are suddenly nothing compared to the ones a distance away from where you live. It takes a whole new perspective on riding to safely ride these roads. It is something you must seriously think about as you ride. Your mind cannot wander; especially when you are in an area you are totally unfamiliar with. There are many threats to your safety out there, especially in turns.

You must be confident in your ability to ride around an object.

Do you know what "Target fixation" is? Target fixation is what happens when your eyes lock onto something in the road, say a bottle or a board or a pile of cow dung, or even a rider that has gone down (crashed) in front of you, and you "Fixate" on it, which does the one thing you did not want to do. It makes you roll right over it. Not good.

How do you avoid doing this? You practice looking where you want to go, not where you don't want to be. See a mark on the pavement; use a pothole for example. Identify it and then look past it, making your motorcycle goes around that hole. You can also set up cones, which are easier, but require the use of a parking lot to do correctly. The idea of using an existing pothole or some variant is that you can practice this while on the go. When you set up in a parking lot you have a controlled environment. It's best to begin practicing things like this in a controlled area. Then graduate to actually doing this in the real world after several days of practice in a parking lot.

One thing to bear in mind with motorcycling is that it takes practice to make perfect. Sometimes you have to do a certain technique twenty to thirty times to get it ingrained where you can perfect it and actually do it right, and even then it may not be correct when you attempt to really apply this technique in daily real-world use.

Turning a motorcycle is one of the most important aspects you must learn about riding one. It sounds easy, but there is a lot to learn to do this correctly, and beyond some belief, just getting on a motorcycle and taking off without any prior thought or road based knowledge almost always ends in an immediate crash.

Go over the basics in your head. Look where you want to go, leave two seconds minimum between you and the vehicle in your same track ahead of you (One second to the vehicle in the other track on a multi bike ride)

Have you ever heard the term "Late apexing?" It is a racing technique that spills over favorably to the real world. This is a good one to learn. Aim your bike towards the outside edge of a turn, then before you pass the center point of that turn, and you begin to have a clear view further up the turn, point the motorcycle to where you want to go. For lean angle junkies this is the only way to do it. For the rest of us a slow entrance with slight acceleration through the turn with a gradual lean angle will suffice. But late apexing works, and is really a must learn for riding.

Motorcycling is one of the most inexpensive and fun hobbies you can have, but it is dangerous, and you must prepare yourself to counter those dangers. Learning to turn correctly is one of the equations necessary.

Don't think it's only high-speed turns that can get you into trouble, it's not. I once saw a rider on a cruiser making a 5 mile per hour corner and dump his bike. His reason? The car in front of him hit his brakes and startled him. Down went the bike and rider. This guy was just a bad rider with no skills. No way should that have happened, ever. He was following too closely, maybe not paying attention, or looking elsewhere, but whatever it was, he went down in front of about a hundred onlookers, and hurt his pride above anything else. (Though I'm not sure of that one because all he was wearing was a leather vest with a pile of pins on it. This is absolutely no protection at all.) You can go down anywhere at any time, you must remember that, and be prepared for something happening in front of you that can affect your ride, and you have to be mentally able to make a quick, decisive decision that can save your life, or at least your hide!

Did you know that improper cornering accounts for more non-lethal motorcycle accidents than anything else? Just so you don't misunderstand, there are an amount of them that are fatal. But there are plenty of low and high-speed crashes caused by improper cornering.

Remember to always look, lean, and roll on the throttle and go. Practice the techniques I outlined previously. Remember to always use them, not just some of the time. You have to make sure they are ingrained into your riding persona and your automatic responses. It's no sin to be slower than the next guy. Being safer is what counts. Become the best you are able to be in corners, but don't be ashamed if there is someone better. Crashing is not learning, sure some will argue that "Whatever does not kill you makes you stronger." But there's no reason to shed blood over this either. A little parking lot practice goes a long way towards making you a better rider.

Remember that there is no trophy at the end

of a ride, there are no umbrella girls and photographers waiting. Ride it like you are enjoying yourself, not like you just stole it!

Chapter Thirteen

"Assume the position!" Huh? What? No, it's not what you think. The position I'm referring to is the lane position. Now we touched earlier on being in the right side or the left side of a lane on multiple bike rides, but when riding solo you should be in the center of the lane, but there are exceptions to that rule too.

When following behind a vehicle you can't see around, such as a van or a pickup truck, it's best to ride the corners. Making sure you are several seconds behind (There's that tactic again!) and in this case, because you won't be able to see above their roofline, off to one side or the other, where you can look and see around these vehicles. You don't know when the vehicle in front of you is going to pass over an old carpet or an opened box of nails. Best to avoid this situation like the plague itself! Be in a lane position to see around the vehicle in front of you, scanning ahead as far as possible and then using that knowledge to safely avoid any road hazard. Also, the best scenario is to simply pass the offending vehicle when the chance allows, which in turn affords you an unobstructed view of the road.

When using entrance or exit ramps, it's best to stay in the center of the lane, using up as much space as possible. You never know when some inconsiderate driver will decide to squeeze in next to you. Don't think it's impossible or unlikely. Neither of those is true. I've seen drivers try to pass me on an entrance ramp. You must take up the entire ramp, or again as much as possible.

Another tactic or technique to practice is "Who is going to take the hit?" What does that mean you ask? Simple. It means whenever you are wary of a situation, position yourself behind a car that will take the impact of any accident, as opposed to you bearing the brunt of it. This is something you should always be thinking about. This should be running in your mind automatically, and again, it's a matter of training to get this right. You have to identify threats to yourself as you ride, constantly. Run things over in your head over and over. "Is that car going to turn left in front of me?" "Does that car's driver even see me?" If you are buried behind larger vehicles and not riding with your high beam on, chances are they DO NOT see you. You can very easily get run over by a driver who did not even realize you were there in the first place.

How do you rectify this? Again, I'll say it over and over, leave at least two seconds between you and the vehicle in front of you, so you are more visible. Always be ready to use your horn. (We'll cover this in a later chapter as I have a lot to say about the anemic things the manufacturers call horns on motorcycles.) Your hands should loosely be wrapped around your grips (Never in a "Death grip") and you should be wide eyed and prepared for whatever may happen. With your hands at the ready, you can brake and clutch simultaneously (Remember we discussed this technique?) You can apply your horn, and you can just assume a more relaxed position on the motorcycle, which is paramount to your riding. By being relaxed, your entire demeanor changes and you can see things in less of a frenetic manner.

Also, NEVER ride next to another vehicle in its blind spot. This is yet another reason to ride in the far-left lane on a multi-lane road. Many drivers just look at their mirrors instead of turning their heads and making sure a vehicle of any sort is not next to them, and even then you could be in someone's blind spot.

The experts all agree that you should always be moving slightly aggressively through traffic. I don't mean you should be lane splitting, revving your engine, and generally making a nuisance of yourself. What I mean is that you should be moving slightly faster than traffic so drivers see and recognize you, instead of you and your motorcycle becoming basically background noise around them. Become recognizable to others. Keep up a speed slightly faster than vehicles around you, and decisively keep your bike moving so that it is not in someone's blind spot. Move your bike in a manner that is fluid and smooth, not jerky and dangerous looking. Best to be thought of as rider that seems to be able to handle his motorcycle with confidence, rather than one that breeds fear and disgust amongst drivers. Always remember there are far more automobile drivers on the roads of America then motorcyclists, even with the rather substantial increase in motorcyclists in the past decade.

Chapter Fourteen

Do you know what the anatomy of a pass is? The anatomy of a pass is simply the structure of how you pass another vehicle. How you put it all together and make it work. Sure there are many out there who will argue you just give a quick look and go, but that's not what it's all about.

To make a proper pass, you have to break it down into sections in your mind. You take each section at a time and then after practicing this, you put it all together.

The first section is why do you want to pass this vehicle in front of you? Are they going to slow? Or are they going to slow for you? That is in truth two different questions that you should think about the answers to.

If they are going at or slightly above the speed limit, and this is annoying you, then they are going too slowly for you. We all know speed limits are falsely written down in this country by the safety-crats as well as the revenuers who love to receive funds from speeding tickets, but the issue is, if that person in front of you is operating in a safe manner, and they are just going to slow for you, then you have to justify it in your own mind if they are worth passing or not.

Now if that person is going slower than the speed limit and just daydreaming, that's another story. In either scenario, you have to justify passing them in your own mind. Once you do that, the rest of the equation comes into play.

You begin to attempt a highway pass by making sure you are leaving plenty of room between yourself and the vehicle in front of you. Then you turn your head and look over your left shoulder (You do know ONLY To pass on the left, correct? Or am I assuming too much?) Once you make sure all is clear behind you, and no vehicle is coming up in the far left lane (Assuming again that you are in the middle lane for some reason.) Turn your left directional on, downshift, stick your left hand out horizontally in the form of a left turn hand signal, grab the left handlebar again, rechecking your mirror, and go. Make the pass cleanly, do not cut off the car you just passed. Give him plenty of room when you drop back in front of him.

If you HAVE to pass in a lane other than the far left (Yes, it does happen. There are plenty of times you'll have some driver doing fifty miles per hour in the far left lane of a highway where the speed limit is sixty five, and he's just holding up traffic as if it was his right.) Look over your right shoulder (Get in the habit of not trusting your mirrors 100%. Use them as reference tools. Mirrors have blind spots.) Turn on your right directional, then downshift. Make the universal arm bent at the elbow pointing upwards vertically sign of a right turn recheck your mirror, and go, again not in a movement that startles or frightens anyone, but in a smooth flow. Leave room to complete the pass, then drop back in line, in front of the vehicle you just passed.

What about passing on a rural two-lane road? This is a bit trickier, but it's not a problem. Again make sure your reason for passing is a legitimate one. At least in your mind. When making this pass you'll be crossing a dotted yellow line and be in oncoming traffic for a short time. So this one you have to be doubly careful about.

Again, leave room ahead of you in case the vehicle in front of you decides to hit his brakes. Turn your head and look over your left shoulder. Make sure another vehicle is not passing both you and the vehicle in front of you that you are attempting to pass.

Left directional on, downshift, now this is the important one: Make sure you have plenty of room to complete your pass. Make sure no cars are coming in the opposite direction, or if they are that they are far enough off that you can complete your pass with plenty of room to spare, and above all safely! Accelerate briskly and leave plenty of room as you pass the vehicle in front of you. Make sure your high beam is on so the vehicle in front of you has a better chance of seeing you attempting your pass. Once past the vehicle in front of you, leave a large enough distance and pull back in front of him, do not cut him off!

Above all, only attempt your pass when the road is straight, not when it is curving or at the bottom of a hill. Straight and flat are what you are looking for, to complete safe passing.

This past chapter is very important, and should be memorized.

One last thing. No matter what, never pass on a double yellow, unless it is an absolute, life threatening necessity. Roads all over the country are falsely marked more and more these days as non-passing zones. They are clear with good visibility and little or no driveways or side roads, yet the municipalities are marking those non-passing zones. There is nothing you can do about it, if you do not live there. Obey the laws, while they are not always right, they are there for a reason. Leave double yellow passing for an emergency situation only, and even then it must adhere to all of the above criteria.

Chapter Fifteen

Complacency breeds bad habits! Yes it does! What do I mean by that? Think about this: If you make a mistake while riding, and it's something you realize is a mistake, and that mistake costs you because you were not stern enough with yourself in your riding, then you are responsible for your own accident.

Think of it this way. Say you want to press down with your left foot on your left peg at every turn. You want to do this, but keep forgetting and you realize afterwards that you forgot, again and again. But instead of enforcing it in your mind that you have to do this, you instead think "I'll get it next time." And the next time, and the next time. But you never enforce this upon yourself. Stop, go back to the spot where you meant to push down on the peg, and this time do it. I'm using the peg technique as an example, but whatever it is, make sure you beat the complacency bug.

It's a good thing to get into certain habits when riding your motorcycle. Make yourself a checklist when getting on the bike. Begin with things like your ear plugs, your gloves, your riding boots, cleaning your face shield before every ride. This stuff should become second nature after a while. Make it happen.

When riding, make sure you practice all of your riding techniques all the time. Make them part of your ride, automatically. Push down and weight the pegs
on every corner. Lean into every turn; push out on

the grips in each direction you are turning the bike in. Don't just acknowledge these practices, do them. Make them part of your riding technique to the point of doing them automatically.

Every time you get out on your motorcycle, make it a practice session. Practice everything you need to know over and over. Go over your weak points, learn to identify them and then work to correct them. Don't just settle for something you know is wrong with your riding. Work to make it right!

Chapter Sixteen

Do you know how to sit on your motorcycle? Silly question right? Not so! You have to be relaxed when on your motorcycle, and not fighting it when it wants to turn or move. You have to become one with it, leaning the way it leans in turns, and just be at ease with the movements on a motorcycle.

Never stiffen up and fight the bike. That's when you'll get into trouble. Keeps your arms loose and bent, and at ease. Use your stomach muscles to hold you up, not your arms and wrists. It takes time to build up the proper muscles to do this. Depending on how you ride, a good part of the season usually. Keep the bike loose under you at all times.

I mentioned earlier not to hold your handlebars in a death grip. Why? Well, it' simple. By starting at your hands and keeping your body the same loose way all the way through, you keep yourself freer and looser to make the bike handle. The key is being relaxed. From head to toe.

So you sit on the bike, using your stomach muscles to hold you up, not your arms and wrists. Keep your head and eyes turning, checking your mirrors, and focusing ahead of you. Your body weight should be on your seat and your pegs.

When you realize you are going to run something over, say a board or something that you know will be a shock to your motorcycle, you place your weight on your pegs and stand up, with your knees slightly bent, getting your weight off of your seat, and onto your pegs.

Keep your mind working and your body

relaxed. Don't tense up when something adverse is happening ahead of you. The trick here is to always be thinking ahead. Like I've said before, leave space and plan your next move before it happens. There's no problem with running "What if?" scenarios through your mind's eye. You should be doing that on a constant basis.

Get used to your motorcycles seat; move around a bit on it when riding. Get comfortable with feeling it beneath you. Learn where your comfortable spot is on your bike. You may have to work a while to find it. But that's okay. Once you do, you'll be set for life. Or at least as long as you have that particular motorcycle.

There are times when you'll have to stretch your legs out on long rides. That's okay, don't be afraid to do that. Push your legs out ahead of you, making sure that your feet are not in a place where they can get caught between your pegs and your bike, breaking your ankle or at least injuring you.

You have to learn about your motorcycle. You have to get comfortable on it. This goes beyond just going out joy riding and looking at the leaves blow in the wind. Put in the time and effort into learning about your motorcycle. Make yourself practice riding techniques. Learn what the seat feels like after a hundred miles of riding. Learn where the most comfortable spot on that seat is. Maybe that seat is no good for your particular build. You may have to go to the aftermarket and buy one that suits you better. Accessories and aftermarket parts will be dealt with later on.

Most importantly though, you have to be

comfortable for some distance on your motorcycle, whatever that may be. If you are a daily rider who uses the motorcycle for commuting, then the bike has to be comfortable for that amount of time. If you are doing five hundred-mile days, then that has to be your consideration. Take all these things into consideration when choosing both a motorcycle and a seat, or seating accessory.

    But more important than that, learn to relax.

Chapter Seventeen

I said relax at the end of the last chapter, but does that only mean to be relaxed in the saddle? No. It means the night before you are doing a big ride (200-500 miles +) make sure you get a full night's sleep. That night is not the night to be out partying like it's 1999! Get your full eight hours of sleep, and wake up refreshed and ready to go the next day. Motorcycling, while not physically tiresome to most, is mentally fatiguing. You end up using lots of mental energy just thinking about what you are doing out on the road.

Consequently, when out on the road, limit your nightly (After you have settled into a room for the night.) alcohol intake. Either don't drink at all, or drink sparsely. Alcohol and motorcycles DO NOT MIX. NEVER drink while out riding. Most fatal motorcycle accidents have alcohol involved. Our sport has been given a stigma concerning alcohol for the past fifty years or so. It somewhere along the way became cool to be the drunken biker with a devil may care attitude. You see cruisers lined up around bars every weekend. Most of these guys ride from their houses to the bar, and then back home again. They are not serious motorcyclists. They are buying into a lifestyle that makes them feel cool. Perhaps their day job is boring and this is their release, but whatever the reason they choose, they are propagating the bad image motorcyclists have acquired over the years.

If you go to a town on a road trip, and the group goes out for dinner (Of course walking to a restaurant), and you decide to have a drink, limit yourself to just one. There's no reason to wake up to a hangover, which will impair your judgment and riding ability more than you realize. You have enough to keep track of while on the road.

So the trick is to be fully alert, and for that, you need a full night's sleep.

But there's more to this then just getting a full nights rest, you have to know when to call it quits for either the day, or for a short rest break. When you are out doing a long distance ride, pace yourself. Know the tell-tale signs that your body needs a break. Don't push yourself to the very limit. That's when disaster can strike!

If you are beginning to feel drowsy when riding, if your attention is not as focused as it was earlier, then you need to take a break. Sometimes all you need is twenty minutes to a half-hour to perk up. Find a nice air-conditioned place to stop in, and relax. In the hot summer months, iced tea (unsweetened) or diet soda is a good bet. Why the sugar free stuff? Sugar makes you sweat more. When it's brutally hot out, the last thing you need is more reason to sweat, and to be uncomfortable. Plain ol' Water works great too, and is actually the very best thing for you. Today, bottled water is available everywhere, so a cold water break is at every gas station, mini mart, and convenience store across the country. You have to replenish lost moisture. It's imperative for your riding, as well as clarity of mind, as much so as getting the proper amount of rest.

Make sure you are nourished as well. Let me share a little story with you concerning nourishment on a motorcycle.

One of my first motorcycle trips was up to Salem, Massachusetts during the Halloween season. A friend's wife said they have this big parade up there that's supposed to be fun to check out. So we decided on a three-day trip up to Massachusetts to check it out first hand. We had breakfast early, say 8 am ish. By 1 O'clock we were still on the highway in traffic, and I was getting hungry. I was persuaded to not eat and to wait till later. Well later never came. We went through rush hour traffic in Boston, found our hotel and promptly decided not to stay there, then finally found another one, and then we finally decided to go see the parade. Well the traffic was bumper to bumper, and the streets were packed. I got separated from my riding companions, while looking for one of us who was missing, and at a light, I dropped the bike, in front of thousands of people. Why did I drop it? I was hungry. I had no more fuel in my tank to keep me going. A guy popped out of the crowd and helped me right the bike, and I promptly dropped it on the other side. I was spent. My body was shot; I had no energy left. I had just spent about 14 hours getting to Salem from New York, and had far too little rest and no nourishment since early that day. If I had stopped when I wanted to and "fueled up" my body, I would have been fine, but sometimes you have to learn lessons the hard way.

The moral here is you know when you require food and rest, not the next guy. Only you can know what is right or best for you when riding. If you need a break, or a bite to eat, or some liquids to keep you sharp, then go get whatever you need. Don't let others decide for you. Learn your limits, and know when to act upon them.

Furthermore, make sure you remain without a doubt the Captain of your own destiny. When you have to stop and take a break, be forceful about it and tell whoever you are with that it's time for you to stop, then just do it. Even a few minutes in the shade with your eyes closed can help refresh you on a hot summer riding day. There are plenty of places available to all of us to take a break. Learn to have the mindset to take advantage of them. Riding is something that should be relaxing, not something that has an intensity and tension to it.

Chapter Eighteen

Early on I mentioned heated clothing for cold season riding. But what about when things are hot? What can you do then? There are several tricks you can use. Remember I mentioned the flow-through jackets in the first chapters? That's the newest option available to us for hot weather riding. Without a doubt, they work. But what else can you do?

There are products out there that look like neck bandana's, but are actually filled with a type of water absorbing crystal, that you soak in cold water for a few minutes, then roll up and wrap around your neck. This will keep you cool for hours. These things work. But there's even a simpler thing you can do.

What is it you may ask? Just go into the bathroom of wherever you are, take your shirt off, and soak it under a cold water faucet. You'll be good for an hour like this and then will have to redo it again. This works VERY well.

What about your legs, you may ask? Wear a pair of breathable, armored over pants, and wear shorts under them. This is so much more comfortable than wearing jeans, and far safer.

What else can you do? Well, wash your face down when you stop with cold water. You'd be surprised how much cooler you feel. I mentioned water in the last chapter, carry a bottle in your tank bag, or luggage. Even splash some on your face if need be.

When feeling like nothing else is working, and you have to get out of the heat, find an air conditioned restaurant and take a good half hour to an hour to cool off while drinking plenty of liquids.

If you are out riding and the heat is unbearable, and you begin to feel a headache coming on, get out of the sun quickly and begin to drink some cool water. You are getting dehydrated and possibly worse at that point. Remember to always take water in slowly when you are feeling like this. Never gulp it down and certainly don't drink it all at once. Let it enter your system slowly.

Several years ago, I was riding with a group of friends from Rochester, NY to Long Island, and the heat of the day was over 100 degrees. We were all wearing full riding gear, and it was like riding into a blow dryer. Suffice to say, we stopped many times on the way home to cool off. One stop took well over an hour at a roadside fast food restaurant, where we drank plenty of fluids and just cooled off.

Again, the key here is pacing yourself. You have to know when to pull over and know when to keep going. It's okay to get home later if need be on a long ride. Getting home safely is the entire battle. Keep your wits about you, and know when to make the call to pull over.

Also, listen to your riding buddies. If they need to pull over, do it. Don't push them into a situation that is dangerous for them. Not everyone tires at the same time, or is as susceptible to the elements as the next guy. What may be tolerable to you, may be beyond someone else's limits, or vice versa.

Chapter Nineteen

Earlier, I spoke of late apexing. Now I'm going to discuss other types of turns. Whether you realize it or not, there are many types of turns out on the roads. The most dangerous of these is called a 'decreasing radius' turn.

What this means is the turn gets tighter the further into it you are. This type of turn can force you to go over the yellow line into traffic, or into the dirt on the shoulder if you do not lean the bike over and counter steer further. These turns come up on your fast, so you have to be mentally prepared to lean over more at less than an instants notice. The decreasing radius is the hardest of turns to master. It's actually best to find one somewhere, then go through it several times in each direction to build up a feel for this type of turn. This will make you confident to ride through this turn and others like it in the future, especially when they come up on you with no notice.

Another type of turn that can sneak up on you is one that is banked or cambered opposite of what it should be. Turns should be banked with the high side of the turn on the outside edge. This is not always so, though. Highway departments and road engineers for some reason barely give this any thought, and while the majority of turns seem to be banked in the correct angle or way, there are some that are banked totally opposite of what they should be. In other words, they will be banked with the high end on the inside of the turn, instead of the outside. This type of turn can throw you off as well as a decreasing radius turn can. Train yourself to recognize these whenever possible.

Now even worse is a combination of the two. And yes, they do exist. You can very easily get a turn that has a decreasing radius and is banked incorrectly. If you go blazing through one of these, chances are you're really in big trouble if you don't realize what is ahead of you.

What are the easy turns? Increasing radius turns are nice, meaning the turn doesn't tighten up as you get further into it, but rather loosens up and becomes easier to handle as you exit it.

A turn that is the same radius all the way through is predictable and nice to roll through. That's probably the easiest one to deal with in any circumstance.

Always remember that you have to be able to see completely through every turn before you can commit to it as far as speed and lean angle go.

How bad can things go if you "overcook" a turn? What does "Overcook" mean even? Well first off, overcooking a turn means you went in too hot, or too fast for the turn or your riding ability. Usually it is a rider's ability that makes a rider suffer, and not his motorcycle, especially a modern sport bike.

Modern motorcycles are so razor sharp that not only will they almost always exceed what an average rider can do with it, they are also almost always hard to manage for an inexperienced rider, or for one who has not ridden sport bikes in the past.

This is the rub with modern sport bikes; they are so good that most are considered twitchy by those unfamiliar with them. This is not a good thing, as it can once again, spook a rider who is not prepared for the actions a top-notch sport bike can give. Modern motorcycles are a far different beast then their older brethren. What only ten years ago was considered a track only weapon can now be out ridden by a sport bike right off today's showroom floor. This is no lie or exaggeration, either! Today's modern machines are just incredible, but the trick is your riding skills have to be up to the task. That is why it is always good to start out as a new rider on something that is not a cutting edge machine.

Getting back to turns, if you are riding a modern sport bike and you are not used to its turning abilities and the reaction time the bike requires (Which is usually far less then you realize) you could end up hurting yourself very easily.

It's always best to make your bike an ongoing lesson every time you ride it. Learn how your bike reacts, no matter what bike you decide to own.

Do you think turns are the only hurdle you'll have to clear? Think again. Even exiting a driveway can be hazardous. If the driveway apron is off camber (Off angle to the pavement surrounding it.) it can be as dangerous as anything else we've spoken of. This can make you turn wide and into the oncoming lane, as well as turn to deep and run into the curb. You have to always have your wits about you, and always keep scanning ahead to see and then do something about whatever hazards may be in your way, including turns that can surprise you very quickly.

One problem some riders seem to fall into is to look

at the ground, and not ahead of them in turns. This is not good. Do you know why? Because as we discussed earlier, where you look, is where the bike is going to go. So aim it where you want it to go and always look that way, not at the ground. If you look at the ground; you'll end up there, especially in a tight turn. You must always pay attention to where you want the bike to be. To accomplish this, your head must be up and staring outwards, not looking at the pavement. Why does this happen? Why do we sometimes stare at the ground? I believe it has to do with the angle of the sport bikes seating position relation to the clip ons (Handlebars).   What are clip ons? Sport bikes do not have true handlebars, which is basically a tubular bar that everything mounts on, including your handgrips, your mirrors, your switchgear (Switches.) A clip on is just a hollow aluminum, or steel tube that is only about half a foot long, and each side of the bike gets one. They weigh less than handlebars and take up less space. They give a sportier feel and image to a motorcycle.

    The new breed of standard style motorcycles all use a regular tubular handlebar as opposed to clip ons. These are considered by many to be adult sport bikes because of their more upright riding position.

    Whatever you decide to ride, put the time and effort into becoming familiar with your motorcycle. Really ride it, not just daydream on it. Recognize things about how your motorcycle reacts in turns, about how the suspension compresses while in turns, about how you are positioned on the seat during these times. Remember to always lean into turns and position your body towards the inside of the turn when at speed, not away from it. There's a lot to learn about turning.

A good thing to do is to go to a parking lot and set up a group of three cones about 20 feet apart. Now ride through them turning slowly from one side to another, first to the right, then to the left side of the second cone, then to the right side of the third. Now decrease the distance by five feet per cone, and do the exercise again. Don't go fast. You'll be better off by taking this slowly, learning how the bike will react to steering inputs. Lastly, drop the cone distances to ten feet between cones and go through that. You'll see the reactions you'll have to make will be more difficult and will require quicker reactions.

Next, see how you'll do this at 30 MPH, start again at the twenty foot distance (By the way, please make sure you're doing this in a dry, clean parking lot without sand.) and slowly move the cones back to ten feet. While doing this exercise, make sure you are looking ahead the entire time, and not at the ground directly in front of you. Scan ahead to the furthest cone when entering the first one. When exiting the last one, scan ahead to where you want to stop the motorcycle. This will help you learn about your motorcycle's reactions to steering inputs as well as your own reaction time.

Chapter Twenty

Carrying a passenger is something you'll end up doing at one time or another in your riding career, whether you realize it or not. This is a whole new aspect of riding you must become familiar with.

Passengers come in all shapes and sizes, from 7 year old kids who weigh all of 50 lbs., to overweight friends who want a ride on the back of your motorcycle. There is a standard mantra they must all be aware of. They must lean the way you lean, and do whatever you are doing. If they lean opposite you when in a turn, the bike will go in the opposite direction you want it to, and this could have dire consequences for all involved!

Passengers should be spoken to before they jump on a motorcycle and explained what is required of them. It's not a free ride, where they can just plop on the seat and do whatever they want to. They have to learn to read what you are doing, and do exactly the same. If you are leaning to the right, they must lean to the right with you. The same goes for leaning to the left. They have to learn to not crowd you on the seat, meaning if they are sliding into you, they have to push themselves back where they belong, in their section of the seat.

Good passengers are hard to find. Most are horrible. I once had one who thought I was leaning too far to the left, so she began leaning to the right, WHILE I was in a turn! I immediately pulled over and told her never to do that again. Her response was that I was leaning too far to the left and it scared her. She never road with me again. That could have become a very dangerous situation that could have hurt both of us. Your passenger must become part of your team when they are riding with you.

There is all kinds of equipment available for passenger riding, including special riding gear for kids from various manufacturers as well as belts that wrap around the riders waist and the passenger puts their hands through, giving them a secure place to hold onto.

The most important thing a passenger needs is a correct fitting helmet. If this passenger is going to be a regular rider with you, sit them down and tell them what they need to buy (If you're not buying it for them). Make sure they get a motorcycle specific jacket, and gloves as well as a helmet that's the right size for them.

If your passenger is a child, chances are you will be changing gear for them once a year, including helmets and jacket. They WILL outgrow what they are currently wearing, and you should be ready to sell last year's gear at the beginning of every season and buy new equipment for your young passenger at the start of every season. Many parents go through years of riding with their child as a passenger, right up to the point where the child gets their own motorcycle, and begins to ride along with their parent.

So what other considerations should you be aware of regarding taking a passenger along? Well, the most important is that passengers require breaks too. Meaning that they need time off the bike as well as you do, but their timetable could very well be different to yours. You have to be aware that your passenger may require bathroom breaks as well as simple time off the bike to stretch their legs. You have to remember that you are riding for two now, and your schedule is going to be different from your passengers.

What items should you tell your adult passengers to purchase? Definitely a helmet if you don't supply one. A riding jacket, gloves and over pants, of course. The last item should definitely be motorcycle (M/C) specific boots, and definitely not a pair of old work boots. No matter what anyone tries to make you believe, those are not acceptable protection in case of an accident.

Your passenger should learn from your example as far as what to wear. Guide them in what gear to buy. Remember, no matter what they say, when they are on the back of your motorcycle, they are ultimately your responsibility. So make them aware of what is expected of them before they throw their leg over your motorcycle. This should be a fun experience for you both, but it should most definitely be a safe one as well. Always remember, and take into consideration that your braking distances are now going to be increased with a passenger on board. Also remember to check tire pressure and whatever you need to top them off.

    But what about those passengers that decide they no longer want to be passengers and that it's time they began riding on their own? I'm glad you asked...

Chapter Twenty One

So now your passenger has graduated to his or her own motorcycle. Are you ready for them to be riding along with you? Make sure they go through everything you did, the MSF (Motorcycle Safety Foundation) training, reading books like this one till they're sick of reading about motorcycles then have them read some more! The parking lot practices, etc.

Now that they are ready to join you on rides, what does that mean for both of you? It means you've just graduated from going solo to becoming part of a group, and of going on group rides. A group is any two or more motorcycles going out for a ride. One thing this does for you immediately is make you more visible, increasing the chances that someone will see both you, and your riding buddy. There definitely IS something to that old adage about safety in numbers!

But what else does this mean on a more personal level?

It means that you must take into account a whole new set of riding rules.

When riding in a group (Two or more motorcycles.) You and others with you have to automatically go into another mind set. You must automatically go into "The Count" (we discussed "The Count" in an earlier chapter.) and keep your at least one second distance from the bike ahead of you. You NEVER ride side by side for any reason whatsoever!

Why not, you ask? It looks cool on TV and you see lots of cruiser guys doing it, right?

Well the reason is simple; it cuts off your escape route on one side just in case something should happen. If you have to swerve to that side in an emergency, you both crash and vice versa. It's not a good thing to ride side by side no matter how cool it looks, it is simply one of the most dangerous things you can do on a motorcycle. Basically, riding side by side is a knucklehead move. Don't be a knucklehead.

So how should you ride then? Well, we already discussed timing, using "The Count", now you have to ride in "The Stagger". No, this is not the same thing that happens when you see cruiser guys leave a bar. That's them just staggering.

"The Stagger" is when you ride in a group (Again that's two or more motorcycles.) and one takes one tire track and the other motorcycle takes the opposite tire track, again at least one second apart.

What are these tire track things I just mentioned? Look at the car ahead of you, see its tires? Well the left side is the left tire track; the right side is the right tire track. You plant your motorcycle in one of those tracks and the other motorcycle goes into the opposite one, riding one second apart.

Now if you have three + bikes they repeat the procedure behind you, so that the motorcycle directly behind you is actually two seconds back from your rear tire.

How big a group can you get like this? It can actually go on theoretically forever. But really the question you should be asking is "How big a group is safe and comfortable?"

Actually, up to about eight motorcycles is about the easiest large group you can get to manage. Anything up to that point is fine.

Now don't get me wrong, I've been riding with large groups three to four times a season for years, and by large I mean 20+ motorcycles. It's almost always safe.

I said "almost always" above, right? Well yes, it is. We've had a few instances of riders having minor accidents, and one instance of a major crash that the rider walked away from.

Accidents DO happen, and the only way to avoid them is to be constantly vigilant in your riding. It's best if everyone in the group adopts this very same mindset. Riders should be entirely focused on their riding, not concerned with someone else in the group (Be it a relative, or friend.)

Now another thing to bear in mind is that these accidents took place over a five-year span of doing group riding.

The point I'm illustrating is that no matter how safe and careful you try to be, things can, and probably will happen that will ruin your day. So you must be ever vigilant (Like that word huh?) with your riding, when riding either in a group or alone.

One way to make sure your group rides are as safe as possible is using good communication between riders. Have a rider's meeting each and every ride before you leave. Gather everyone together at your meeting spot, and tell them what's expected of them. Tell them about "The Count" and how to use it to ensure proper spacing. Tell them they must always maintain at least two seconds between their motorcycle and the one directly in front of them, and one second to the one in the other track ahead of them.

Next, explain to them that while it's really nice to see all the pretty colors, it's nicer still to remain alive, so tell them they have to maintain their attention on their riding, not the trees or the waterfalls or (better yet) the pretty girls walking on the sidewalk or whatever they are passing.

Finally, make sure they are riding with proper gear. I personally won't ride with anyone who wears a beanie helmet (those things are only good for serving chips out of, with salsa on the side) I also won't ride with anyone who does not wear an M/C (Motorcycle) specific jacket. No dungaree or Jean jackets allowed! Ditto for those leather vests. Riders must be in proper gear at all times to ride safely. If they go down (Crash) and get seriously injured because of lack of gear, it ruins everyone's afternoon, not just their own. It's a very selfish mark on the rider who does not care what his lack of skill and preparedness does to those he rides with.

    Consequently, his motorcycle should be well maintained as well. Take a look at the motorcycles of those you ride with when doing group riding. Do their tires look low on air? Tell them that. Don't be afraid to voice your opinions to them. Do their bikes look unsafe? Start at the top and just casually go over a motorcycle that for some reason rubs you the wrong way. You'll be able to tell this soon enough on your own. Something about it will not click with you. Either you'll see oily spots under it, or the aforementioned tires will not look right (Check for cracks and tire rot! Especially on older motorcycles!) If someone's headlight or brake and taillights do not work, make them either fix it on the spot, or send them home. There are too many stories out there about motorcyclists getting into accidents because of another rider's inattentiveness.

    The worst accident I've ever seen took place when a rider on an ST1100 went into a curve very hot behind another rider. The motorcycle two positions up innocently tapped his brakes before the curve to scrub off some speed. The rider behind him did the same, but the last rider panicked because he had not left enough room between himself and the rider ahead of him. He locked his brakes and went into a guardrail, destroying his motorcycle in seconds flat, and earning himself a helicopter ride to the hospital.

He emerged fine and was home the next day, but his experience could have culminated in a far worse way.

Group riding is, as far as I'm concerned the most fun you can have when riding a motorcycle. I personally love the camaraderie it instills, and it's just plain fun to be around others of like mind where you can compare notes on the days ride as well as simply enjoying shooting things back and forth between yourselves. But it can also be the most dangerous type of riding. Something to bear in mind at all times.

Group riding is not a macho excuse to show the group your stuff, and "wick it up". (Meaning ride at 100% of your ability.) Again when you see someone who is hot-dogging it in front of the group and just generally showing how immature a rider he really is, tell him flatly it's time for him to leave. There is no reason for anyone to get hurt because of this person's lack of riding sense. That's not what group riding is about.

Now true, there are sport bike groups that go out every weekend all across the country and scrape foot pegs wherever they can. I myself believe this is foolish and gives the sport another black eye it does not need. I ride sport bikes, but I never abuse them, as so many do. Hey, let's be honest, everyone is going to see how fast their motorcycle feels at a one time or another. I have never pushed mine to the limit. I don't believe that just because a motorcycle is able to do 150 mph that you should verify that fact on public roads. Not only will you get a ticket and probable jail time, loss of license, large fines and general other problems that will make your life miserable for years to come, but if someone does this in a group setting, he jeopardizes everyone else's riding for that day as well as the foreseeable future.

The officer who pulls this rider over will gladly hand out tickets for whatever violations he finds on everyone else's motorcycle, real or imagined!

Another good tool to use when group riding is a radio communication device, but these should only be used by the riders in the group who have the most experience and are considered the most competent. Communicators allow those up front (The group ride leaders.) to warn others of road conditions as well as when a certain turn is coming up or (Heaven forbid!) a downed rider. They also make group riding easier for those who need to take a break from the seat for a few minutes and to communicate that back or forwards to their fellow riders.

All in all, communicators make group riding more pleasurable and far easier than it is without them.

But what do you do if your riding buddies do not have communicators? Work out hand signals. Use the standard left hand all the way out, horizontal and pointing to the left for turning left or moving to the left lane. Point your left hand straight up while bent at the elbow for a right turn. Use the left hand pointing at the ground, again bent at the elbow for "stopping"

There are other hand signals you can work out as well. You can find descriptive files of them on the Internet at http://www.ridemyown.com/articles/safety/handsignals.shtml.

Now what about actually riding in a group? We already mentioned the "Stagger", so we know that is a must, but what about cornering? How do we go about that while staggered? We don't. When entering a corner, everyone moves to the center of the lane, and takes the turn in the center of the lane, allowing themselves ample room for error to either side. I also recommend increasing your distance to the bike in front of you to the full two seconds when entering a turn, so that again means (I know we hit on this before!) doing your braking before the turn, and slightly powering through the turn to make the rear of the bike squat down, and gain the utmost traction. Now with a group using this technique, you spread out slightly before a turn, or curve in the road (Which is what I really mean, and not an out and outright or left-hand turn.) and close up your ranks again when you all move through the turn.

That's the way it should be done. You should never be riding side by side, and you should never be riding in a competitive manner through the turns or corners with no distance (Error cushion) between motorcycles.

You need an error cushion at all times, especially in the curves.

By the way, when talking about riding with fellow motorcyclists you'll hear the word "Cornering" used quite a bit. Cornering is what we do when we ride through curves. It's the most common term used to describe riding through corners, curves or "twisties", which is another term used to describe corners.

Another thing to keep in mind when riding twisties is the placement of the motorcycle in the curve. Why do I say it's important to keep your bike in the center of the lane with plenty of spacing fore and aft? If you hug the center lane and you're leaned over in a corner or turn or twisty or whatever you want to call it, chances are your head will be over the double yellow line, and into oncoming traffic. What could happen then, and HAS happened to others is both horrible to witness and life ending for the rider. Always move to the center of the lane in corners and space yourselves out.

Group riding is fun! When you see several bikes twisting magically through a mountain pass, it's truly a thing of beauty. The trick is learning how to do it, and to plan it correctly, and that requires work.

Chapter Twenty Two

How do you plan a ride? Do you know where to begin? Well pilgrim, I'm here to tell you how right here and now.

If you are going on a day ride, or longer, the best way to start is not just to hop on your bike and roll away, though there are times when that's a pretty darned good way to start the day. No the other way is to simply plan ahead. Create a destination you want to get to, and depending if it's a day ride or a weekend or longer trip, plan your destination(s) out, with areas to make stops at along the way.

Now sometimes you have no idea what lies in your path, no idea where the rest areas are or where you can find a bathroom to even stop at. The best way to deal with this is to ask riders in your area if they've ever been to a certain area you are heading to. Motorcyclists are a nomadic lot. We travel a lot. People you know may have inside information on where to go and how to get there and what is nearby and useful to you.

Like I've said before, join an Internet based riding group for your local area and learn all you can from those members.

Groups like the "LIME Longriders" (WWW.LIMELongriders.info), or the "Sportriders of New England" (www.sportriders.com) or the "Sportbikes of New York City" (WWW.SportbikesofNYC.org) You'll find a deep well of information on all things motorcycling in each of these groups, and many more like them across the world wide web. One word of caution, if you see that a group is popularizing squidly riding, or stunting, move on. They are not a responsible group. None of the above mentioned groups are in any way a bad influence on motorcycling. All of them are responsible.

Getting back to planning, decide on a destination, plan on how you are going to get there whether you are going on back roads, or "slabbing" it (taking the highway) and plan your stops accordingly.

A great thing about a destination is that you know where you're going to be at the end of the day. It's very easy to do 350 miles in a day and end up back home or that distance away for the evening. Some rides turn into 500+ mile days, and don't doubt that you'll be doing this. If riding gets into your blood, anything is possible.

It helps to have maps made out explaining where you should be at any given time, give or take some time of course. Always have a cell phone with you for emergencies, especially if traveling alone.

But that's not the only thing you'll need to have on your motorcycle for other than local riding.

What other items should you have handy? Oh I have a list for you!

Make sure you have a flashlight (Mini mag style lights are great to have in a tank bag) A tire gauge is very important, as is a simple pen and pad. A spray on cleaning solution for your face shield is very important, as well as a few rags and if you have a chain drive motorcycle, you'll need a small can of chain lube as well.

One other item you should have on your

motorcycle at all times, whether on a trip or not, is a spare headlight bulb. Be familiar with how it is changed also. I have had to change headlight bulbs several times while out on the road, so this is a cheap necessity to have under your seat.

My tank bag also contains two pairs of gloves at all times, one slightly heavier than the other, depending on the season.

What other things are needed for your away from home excursions? Some of this stuff is not necessary, but it helps to keep the curious and the nefarious away from your prized possession. In one of your saddle or tail bags, put a long cable style lock that can go through several motorcycle rims at the same time, locking more than one motorcycle together.

This is the most effective way to keep your motorcycle your own. Locking several motorcycles together makes it more difficult for the would be thief to make off with one. Make sure you have an additional disk lock in your tank bag as well, so you can have the cable go through your rear wheel and the disk lock on your front wheel overnight. Just make sure you remove BOTH before you leave in the morning.

Another optional item to have along is a motorcycle cover. Now there are many various manufacturers of motorcycle covers out there, and they come in all shapes and sizes too. Find the right one for your motorcycle that folds as flat as can be and can fit in your luggage without taking up too much room. The reason for taking a cover along is twofold. One, if there are prying eyes, attached to the curious who want to sit on a motorcycle, or worse yet, have their child sit on a motorcycle (This happens all the time, believe it or not.) that is not their own, this will deter them. Also, the obvious reason for carrying a cover on an overnight trip is weather related. If it rains, your bike is dry in the morning. This means you're not sitting in a puddle for the morning ride.

    Another good item to have in the tank bag or side bags is a bottle of water, as mentioned earlier.

    Yet another new toy to bring along is a GPS unit (Global Positioning Satellite) which can make route maps for you as well as tell you where you are and how to get there from here! Many long distance motorcyclists use GPS units and refer to them as if they were their lifeline. They are a good investment for those that like to travel, and take a lot of the guesswork out of trip planning. You can find hotels, restaurants (By name!) and many, many other points of interest with a GPS unit attached to your handlebars.

    But don't become complacent. GPS's are just machines and as such are fallible. There are many stories of people following GPS routes to end up on dirt roads or less! So keep your heads up and be wary of roads suddenly turning to dirt under a GPS's guidance! Otherwise it's a great tool to have, and the benefits far outweigh the faults!

    Using a GPS on a group ride is just another way to make a ride go easier, with less likely problems. When the GPS owner plots the ride out the night before, he then leads the ride and everything should work out properly, or at least easier than it would have without the GPS. It's but one more tool to make our trips work for the better.

Make sure you find out what everyone's motorcycle can get mileage-wise out of a tank full of gas. This is very important. If you have someone in the group who only gets 125 miles out of a tank, you know you have to be looking for gas at or before the 100-mile mark.

Consequently, if everyone can get 200 miles per tank full, then you're good to go at least 100+ miles before you have to stop, and usually at least 150 miles.

One suggestion, if you stop at a gas station and you're at the 100 mile mark, and you feel you can still go another 100 miles before filling up, fill up anyway. Don't let unknown roads and uncertainty of where a gas station down the road may be ruin your groups ride. Believe me, this can ruin the day for everyone. You'll end up with five different riders going in five different directions looking for a gas station for you, leaving you on the side of the road alone. After sometimes two hours of this you'll get everything settled and back together before resuming. That's a MAJOR chunk of your day. And of course after this, everyone will want to stop somewhere and de-frazzle for a while. More time wasted. Fill up often. If you have one guy in the group who is grouching about this because his motorcycle gets 300 miles per tank full, tell him to go on ahead and the rest of the group will meet him at the destination. This will either quiet him down, or he will leave. Either way the problem is solved.

Another thing to bear in mind when doing

group rides is how far a rider can go before needing a rest. Now there are some people out there who can do 100 miles at a clip easily. The other side of the coin are the people who can only ride 50 miles before needing to get off their motorcycles. To be honest, that person needs to get out more, and build up a better seat time, because now he will hinder your riding time, but you have to be accommodating to that person at first at least.

Everyone's situation is different. Myself, I have to go 90+ miles just to get to the nice riding. Living in an area accessible only by bridges and long flat miles of slab is not the place a motorcyclist wants to be. Yet it is reality that some of us do have to traverse cities or miles of highway to get to the scenic twisty bits.

Leading a group to these areas takes planning, and knowledge of the riding group. Meaning get to know each other if you are going to be regular riding buddies. Spend a little time together discussing motorcycles, discussing how you all like to ride, what are your preferred road types (Highway, back road, etc.) Discuss riding gear, tires, and proper riding technique. Make it a social event, as well as a riding event. Meet once a week for coffee or breakfast or dinner even. Get to know each other.

Planning is everything on a group ride; it's no longer just you and your own personal considerations off and away for a few days or longer. Now you have to account for anywhere from one to seven+ other people along as well. You have to know (If you are the group leader) how to space your stops, what pace the group should be riding, and where you will stop for the day.

This and many more considerations that could pop up at a moment's notice are what are in involved in planning a group ride. It's not just jumping on your motorcycles and away you all go.

Time and effort should be put into running a group ride.

Another good tool for group riding, beyond the GPS is getting some form of mapping software, like "Microsoft streets and trips" or its equivalent and creating route sheets for the leader to follow if need be. Bear in mind the only one doing this should be a polished and longtime rider, as he will be looking down at his tank bag an inordinate amount of time to follow a route. This in and of itself can be dangerous, but the proper amount of preparation can make this an easy thing to accomplish. Simply make sure someone who has done this before leads the group, and make sure that person has read the route through several times prior to leaving, so he has parts of it embedded in his memory, and a quick scan of it will remind him where the next turn is.

Most important on a group ride is to find a pace that makes the slowest, most inexperienced person in the group comfortable. If that is to slow a pace for others then break the group up into two halves and send the faster guys going, and let the more leisurely guys just meet them there.

Always remember to ride your own ride. That is the single most important axiom in motorcycling, and bears memorizing, especially on group rides when egos may flare. Again, watch for this to happen, and nip this problem in its proverbial bud by whatever means necessary. Anyone who tries to create an atmosphere of friction or at least competitiveness on a group ride does not belong on that or any group ride. He belongs on a track.

I remember a few years back at that years Americade rally in the Adirondack mountain region of New York State, a riding buddy and myself had signed up for a manufacturer sponsored group ride and dinner with about 50 other riders. I was riding my Yamaha YZF600R and my friend was riding his Kawasaki ZZR1200. Most of this group was made up of mature riders who were on touring, sport touring, or cruiser style motorcycles, of varying makes. Along came a rider, who was in his fifties if he was a day, riding a 600cc sport bike that was done up with custom touches here and there. The motorcycle was very nice looking, but this fellow just had me aware of him by his rather cocky nature.

The ride itself was some hundred miles in length through scenic back roads, over reservoirs, and through quiet wooded areas. When this fellow had enough of the sedate pace he asked my friend and I if we would like to go on a sport bike ride with him. We declined, and so he and one other rider took off and disappeared like they were on fire. At the next stop, the ride organizers approached my friend and me and thanked us for not joining these guys, and adding to the ruination of the planned ride.

Yes, that ride was more sedate then I would have liked, and yes there were a lot of people there moving slowly through towns, but this was not annoying, it was just different. It was a chance to take in the scenery, and make new friends. Were there other people who lacked riding skills in certain areas? Definitely. Many there had no idea how to ride in a group ride situation. They were all over the lane, forcing those behind them to switch lane positions on a moment by moment basis, and this went all the way back up the line to the end.

But in the end when that rider came up to me at the restaurant that the ride organizers had brought us to, and asked why I had not joined his sport bike ride, I politely told him I was there for the group ride and dinner event that I had paid for, and wanted to see that till its finish. He could not understand that, but that's okay too.

What he was going to do was going to be a full out, pedal to the metal squid-fest on public roads, with lots of high speed hijinks and other foolish behavior so he could prove his manhood to others. I wanted no part of that, and graciously declined. All of that was a recipe for a possible disaster.

This is the perfect example of a rider who does not fit the group ride mentality. He was bored almost immediately, and wanted out. He could not sit still in an environment that he felt did not showcase his riding style. While he may have been a nice guy, which remains to be seen, he was a detriment to those around him who wanted a more sedate day ride in the country.

Bear in mind also that the people who were moving all over the lanes were also a problem that needed resolving. They were spoken to by others in the group and given riding pointers at a stop along the way. This was done diplomatically as to not insult anyone, but to also keep the ride safe for everyone else.

The point of the previous paragraphs was to illustrate the kind of riders who do not fit in with the group ride philosophy, and others who have deficiencies in those areas, but who can be instructed on how to repair those deficiencies.

Keep in mind that not everyone is built for group riding, but that's something that they have to realize, not just you. If they are a problem, and you feel they are unsafe to those around them, then the ride leaders should speak to them quietly and tell them either to shape up or ship out.

Chapter Twenty Three

Now you're a seasoned rider, and you have a group of riding buddies who enjoy long weekend rides as much as you do. But how do you lead a ride like this?

You have to learn to think for others, no longer just yourself. You can't just jump out into traffic when you see a spot opening up any longer. It's not just one motorcycle that has to cross the road. It's now several you have to plan for. This brings us to this; talk to your riding buddies before each ride. I mentioned ride meetings earlier prior to each ride. Well this is where you discuss things like pulling out into traffic and what is expected of each rider. If someone gets insulted about discussing what is expected of them, explain to them this is for the good of everyone on the ride, including themselves. If they still don't like it, let them go their own way.

One thing you don't want is for riders to block intersections and hold up traffic. This is something to think about. Many of us have seen big groups of riders purposely hold up traffic while crossing roads. One rider will pull out and stop traffic, and then he waves everyone past him.

This is a bad idea, and should never be done. It annoys drivers who now have to stop their daily pace and let a bunch of nervy "bikers" out in front of them. Not only does it annoy other motorists, but it also is blatantly dangerous. All you need is for one driver who is not paying attention to not realize you are stopped, and you end up with a multi vehicle collision that ends up with a motorcyclist hurt or dead, and several other people's lives hurt or ruined.

Blocking the road is foolish and can only lead to trouble. Don't do it with your riding group.

Learn who is responsible and whom you can trust in your group. Place that person at the tail to ride "sweep".

Riding "sweep" is a term used to describe the rider who is in the last position. The sweep rider keeps an eye on everyone ahead of them, and through the use of a communicator lets everyone know that there may be a problem behind them, or even up ahead, via a warning from the lead rider.

Sweep riders are very important to good riding groups. They are as a responsible part of the equation as are the lead riders, and should be chosen wisely.

What other things should lead riders discuss with the rest of his group? How to leave from any point the group is stopped at is a good starting point.

The ride leader should wait until there is a sufficient opening for several motorcycles at once to get out, and the riders in the group should be informed enough beforehand to know when not to pull out in traffic, when to use their heads and know where to cut off from the others, and await another chance to merge with traffic.

Consequently, the rest of the group, including the ride leader, should know to take their time and to wait for the others to catch up. At this point the ride leader should keep the group in the right lane, moving slow enough for the others to catch up, but not slow enough to be bogging down traffic either.

When everyone is back together (In an orderly fashion, not everyone all over the place in some hectic, frantic mish-mosh.) the group moves to the left lane and returns to moving slightly faster than traffic, as to not hold up any other traffic in the left lane.

Know your fellow riders. Know their riding limits and when the group should stop. When riding in a group, you should have a relaxed pace and ease your way through your ride. Remember that a group ride (Especially one with more than just a couple of riders) is not a marathon, or a race. That kind of riding should be reserved for track days. Just take it in a relaxed, comfortable for all pace, and see the sights, but don't obstruct traffic either. The lead and sweep riders have the responsibility of keeping things in check. But every other rider has the responsibility of keeping himself safe, as well as those around him. No one is responsible completely for others, we all have to assume responsibility for ourselves and act accordingly. That means being responsible in our group riding, and not expecting others to pick up the pieces in case something should happen. Always ride as if you yourself are responsible for your actions, and as though you do not want to inconvenience those around you.

When riding alone, there's no one there to help you in case something should happen. But when riding in a group you have others to help you out in case of something like an accident, or even a breakdown in the middle of nowhere. But make no mistake; it is an inconvenience to those around you. That should make your riding in a group more responsible, at the very least if not more so when riding alone.

The ride leader has to know his rider's strengths and weaknesses. If one rider has a back problem, for example, and requires more stops then the rest, that's fine, and the rest of the group has to realize this.

What I'm trying to say here is that groups should ride in an "All for one and one for all" mentality, and it's up to the ride leader to impart this.

But it's also up to the rest of the members of the group not to ride in a manor detrimental to everyone else in the group.

So tell your riding group that you're not their baby sitter, and they have to ride smart when riding as a group.

When riding with a smart, safe riding group led by a smart, safe leader who imparts his practices and theories to the rest of the group, the ride itself becomes something that's not stagnant, not haphazard and not disorderly or dangerous. A group ride should be a precise event. It should not be filled with teeth grinding nervousness. It opens up the doorway to all kinds of fun and camaraderie, and this is what group riding is all about!

Chapter Twenty Four

Now we're going to breach a subject that no one wants to discuss, but should be discussed by everyone. It's not something that's going to go away and it could have a very important impact on each of us someday, at any given moment. What do we do in case of an emergency?

The very first thing we should learn to do is not to panic. If a fellow rider has an accident, someone (Preferably more than one person) has to remain calm and have a cool head.

Go over the basics. Is the person conscious? Are they breathing? Are they bleeding?

What I am about to say here is the single most important thing NOT to do in case of a motorcycle accident. NEVER remove the helmet of a downed rider. I repeat, NEVER remove their helmet. If they have received some sort of neck injury, by you removing their helmet, you could paralyze them for life. Wait for EMT's (Emergency Medical Technician's) to arrive on the scene and let them determine if the rider's helmet is okay to remove. DO NOT let the rider up off the ground. More than likely they are in shock, and do not realize the extent of their injuries, if any.

Immediately after checking the rider's condition pull out your cell phone and call for help. If you cannot get a signal where you are, and there is a house nearby, go to that house and have them call for help on their hard line. If you are in the middle of nowhere, and there are more than two of you present send someone out a few miles and have them check for a working cell signal if you cannot get one where you are.

If the rider is bleeding, do what you can to stop or slow the bleeding as much as possible. Use tourniquets to stem the flow of blood. Have a rider move down the road and get off of his motorcycle, and direct traffic around the accident scene. Chances are, Police and Fire emergency vehicles will arrive quickly, and they will take over from there. Make sure the rider is as comfortable as possible, but do not move his neck and head at all. Do not raise or lower his limbs, as to not move anything in his neck and back, avoiding permanent injury.

Try to comfort the person as much as possible until the EMT's arrive, then stand back, but make sure you are aware of everything that happened prior to, and immediately after the accident. They will ask you questions such as "Was he awake or unconscious after the accident?" It's important that you know the right answers.

The aftermath of this will be that your entire group will be shaken and nervous. When your friend is taken away by ambulance, you should immediately move everyone to a safe place where they can relax and try to calm down. Nerves will be shattered and people will be in bad shape after this, mentally. Try to remain clam, Get everyone to a coffee shop or diner, and let them get off their motorcycles and relax for an hour or two. After all, you still have to get home from wherever you are.

After everyone has calmed down, however long this may have taken, you can begin your ride home. Someone should take command and lead the others, keeping the speed of the ride down, and making it as comfortable a ride as possible for everyone going home. Hopefully there will be more than just one of you who will have been able to keep his head. If so, and you have another rider you can depend on, move him to the back of the pack and let him ride sweep. Hopefully you both will have communicators and he will be able to keep you apprised of the rest of the group.

The important thing to do in this situation is to keep everyone calm, and to reflect that calm yourself. You do not want to be 200 miles from home, and have to ride back with a half dozen other shaken riders. If things are that bad, suggest that you all take motel rooms for the night. In the morning everything will be better, and people will have a clearer head for the ride home.

Chapter Twenty Five

Have you ever seen motorcycle racing on TV, or at a live event? Has it inspired you? Do you want to ride like these pro racers do? Well first and foremost you have to realize that riding on a track is not like riding on the street. Tracks are clean and clear of debris. There are no cars; there are no dogs or children running into the road. There are no branches and other tree parts hidden around a curve, and there are no Police officers hiding behind a bush with a radar gun. On a track, you can go as fast as you'd like to go, and no one can tell you no.

But like anything else with motorcycling, you have to learn first. How do you learn how to ride on the track? You do track days. Track days are basically classes held on the racetrack, with professional level instructors, who are also club or pro level racers.

One thing to always remember when doing track days, only take a motorcycle to the track that you don't mind throwing on the ground. Accidents can and do happen. Not all the time and it's not guaranteed. But there are times that you take a chance on crashing, or someone crashing into you.

Now the upside of all this is that there are ambulances on the track at all times. So in case you do sustain an injury, medical help is mere seconds away, instead of long and frightening minutes.

Listen to the teachers. Ask questions. That is what they are there for. The instructors are skilled professional racers who have many hours of track experience. They can show you the correct lines to follow and help you in many ways by following you around the track, and critiquing your riding.

Riding on a track opens up a whole new sensory perception for you. Your mind is focused only on the motorcycle and the track before you. No more worrying about obstacles and road imperfections. Just go out there and ride hard.

There are certain things you need to do for a track day, to get your motorcycle ready. Most times you have to tape up the headlight and the remove the mirrors, you have to safety wire the oil filler cap and drain plug, among other things. (What is safety wiring? It's when you drill small holes in these items and others and run a length of braided safety wire through them, then tying that wire off so no parts can come loose and scatter onto the track.)

Safety wiring is also for the containment of fluids (Oil, water, and brake fluids.) should a component containing those fluids come loose. Most track day organizations do not call it a mandatory requirement that your motorcycle be safety wired; though they do suggest or encourage it, sometimes strongly.

Complete instructions can be found at any track day organization's website. Make sure your tires are in good shape. This is an important one! You also must remove the license plate and a few other items.

What should you avoid on the track? Avoid any twenty-something kid who thinks he's Nicky Hayden. He's an accident waiting to happen. Pull into the pit area for a minute and let him get past you and halfway around the track then go back out. Track days are not races, they are schools. You are going there to learn to make yourself a better rider. One benefit of doing track days is that you will learn how far your machine can lean into curves when cornering. This way in case you are ever put into a situation on the street where you have to lean further, you will not freeze up and grab huge amounts of brake lever. You will ease the bike further into the turn and go down as much as you need to, allowing yourself and your motorcycle to compensate for the turns imperfections.

You will also learn the limits of braking on your particular motorcycle. Another very useful tool relevant to the street.

Riding on the track will also teach you how to be smoother on the gas and brakes, as well as how to position your weight properly for cornering. These are all items everyone can use. I'm not saying you have to do track days, but it's an option for learning how to be a better rider.

Track days are held by organizations all across the country, and usually there are organizations that hold several during a season at a certain track, or their home track.

There are also full-blown race schools that hold track events. These are for those that really want to go fast, and are thinking of trying racing in the near future.

What do you need to do to prep yourself for a track day? Make sure the track day organizations safety gear requirements are met. In other words, if you only have a Cordura riding suit, does that meet track day requirements by the holder of the event? Most times the answer is yes, but in some organizations it's leather only. Best to find out beforehand.

One thing to bear in mind is that track days are an expensive proposition. They can cost anywhere from two hundred dollars per day to over a thousand, depending on the organization that is hosting it.

Another consideration is that your motorcycle must be transported there on a trailer, or truck, and not ridden. The reasons? It has to be track prepped first off, and secondly it has to be able to be taken home in case of a crash.

Some riders who do several track days a year only ride on the track. They consider street riding to dangerous. This is all a matter of perspective I believe, and depends on what they want to get out of a motorcycle, and motorcycling in general.

Find out more about track days by searching

on the Internet on sites like ww.tonystrackdays.com , www.NESBA.com, or www.teampromotion.com.

Chapter Twenty Six

What useful accessories can you purchase for your motorcycle? Well there is an aftermarket plethora of items available, a veritable cornucopia of trinkets and do-dads for just about every motorcycle made. You can buy things from chromed, or color matched tire valve caps to carbon fiber body panels and everything in between to dress up your motorcycle.

But what are the good items to acquire? The ones that make sense and have a real use? There are actually plenty of them.

Start simple. Buy yourself a good tank bag (Or a simple set of saddle bags if you're a cruiser rider.) so you can stow some gear for riding. You can put your baseball cap, your sunglasses, your gloves and whatever else in there, including a sweatshirt for inclement weather. Buy yourself a nice tire gauge, with a hose and a push button release on it. Several manufacturers make them like this, and the hose allows easy access to both valve stems.

There are several aftermarket kits for sale that turn your rear turn signals into running lights. I add these to every motorcycle I purchase. You can be seen far better in both nighttime riding and daylight, as you now have three times the light at the rear of the motorcycle as you did. Why there is not a federal motor vehicle law that requires all three rear lights on a motorcycle to be on as running-stop lights is beyond me. But for about $40 and a half-hours time you can wire this set in yourself, and make your motorcycle MUCH more visible.

Well they can see you from the rear now, what about the front? Get an aftermarket headlamp. The stock bulb in a motorcycle is 55/60 Watts. Meaning a 55-watt low beam, and a 60-watt high beam. There are bulbs out there that go to 90/100 watts of power. Depending on the motorcycle though, you run the risk of melting the wiring harness or the reflector inside the headlamp housing itself. There are other choices out there that use new gasses to make brighter headlamps. Look into all your alternatives in the aftermarket and decide what is best for you. Bear in mind that some of today's motorcycles use two 55/60 W bulbs in one housing for a bright swath of light. These headlamps need no tweaking. It's usually the single bulb set ups that require a little help.

What about seeing YOU better at night? How about a stylish helmet halo? This is a rubberized band of reflective material that wraps around the bottom of your helmet, and is VERY bright at night when headlamps are turned upon it. The safety gains are astronomical with a helmet halo in place on your helmet.

You can also buy reflective tape in sheets and cut out whatever pattern you would like for the back of your helmet. Either way, adding some sort of reflector to your helmet is a great idea to improve the ability of others to see you, and to make you more conspicuous. In most states, it's also the law.

Another anemic part of any motorcycle is its horn. This can be easily remedied by a quick trip to any auto parts store. Just pick up a car horn set to the high frequency. (Cars usually have two horns, a low frequency and a high frequency. The high is better, louder and more piercing, it'll get attention.) Depending on the motorcycle this shouldn't take any real time to install.

We've already touched on aftermarket seats earlier in this tome, but to refresh, look around out there in the rear of any major motorcycle magazine. There are tons of seat options available to you. There are companies that rebuild your existing seat to your specifications; there are ones that will outright build you a new seat (Including the seat pan.) You can make any motorcycle comfortable, you just have to have available money to make it work as these seats can run over a thousand dollars depending on what you have done. The average seat replacement/rebuilding runs around the $200-300 mark.

Do you want your motorcycle to stand out in a crowd? Then start hunting through the Internet and catalogues for carbon fiber parts. There are huge amounts of carbon fiber replacement parts available for your motorcycle. Dash plaques, engine covers, license plate frames, triple tree covers, the list goes on and on, and every one of them look great!

Carbon fiber not your thing? How about color anodized aluminum? You can get matching blue, red, even yellow anodized pieces for all the popular motorcycles, and most of these items are universal for several different motorcycle models and makes (Such as for brake fluid reservoir covers.) There are chain guards available in anodized, there are rear huggers, and there are many, many colored options available to all.

What about windshields? Windshields or windscreens as they are referred to by some manufacturers, are available in all shapes and sizes. You can get some that have an upturned lip that changes airflow; you can get a screen that has a double curve to it, a sort of "Double bubble" that improves airflow with a more modern shape. There are windscreens available that are colored to stylishly match a motorcycles paint scheme. All of these are great choices and serve to individualize your motorcycle to your tastes.

There are aftermarket exhaust systems for every make and model of motorcycle made. While I don't condone open pipes, the average aftermarket exhaust that doesn't fry the ears of the person driving behind you ain't so bad. In fact, some of them sound downright cool.

BUT... you have to choose the right one for you responsibly. Don't get one that is so loud you annoy everyone around you. Purchase one that sounds throaty and husky, but does not wake the dead every time you pass a cemetery.

What other kinds of accessories can you get for your motorcycle? How about tank protectors? These come in either black or color matched for every make and year of sport bike out there. There are even clear plastic ones that come precut to your tanks shape. All you do is peel it off and apply, and you are done!

Do you know what frame sliders are? They are the round plastic cylinders that stick out of the frames of many newer sport bikes these days. Not only are they kind of neat looking, they actually serve a purpose, and will protect the frame and some of your plastic in the event of you crashing your bike in a low side accident. They are inexpensive too. They are good insurance for the frame and side panels of your motorcycle.

What if you want to go on a long trip, like we previously spoke of? You'll need luggage, correct? There are many saddle and tail bag manufacturers out there that offer bags in every shape, color and size. Again, look to the Internet and magazine pages for all the info you need on everything that is available for your motorcycle. There are bags in a flowing shape that run with modern sport bike lines, there are large bags you can easily carry far more than just a sparse few items for longer trips. Look to companies like Chase-Harper, Tour Master, Joe Rocket, Nelson-Rigg, and many more for your travel and luggage needs.

There are also hard luggage choices made by Givi, Corbin, Hepco & Becker and several more manufacturers out there. Hard bags have the advantage of being waterproof. They remove easily, but their downside is the always-there mounting brackets that become a permanent part of your motorcycle.

One other option is the Ventura rack system that mounts a tall, large double-sided bag to the rear of the motorcycle on a removable rack. It holds large amounts of gear and clothing and is not objectionable to look at as everything removes quickly when the bag is not in use.

The options for luggage are out there and useful for everyone.

All it takes is some searching on these manufacturers' web sites, or the web site of a motorcycle accessory company to find just what you need. A little research on your part will help you find the set up that is perfect for your particular situation.

What other accessories can use on your motorcycle? The sky is the limit with most modern motorcycles. There are all kinds of colored handgrips made of a gel material to help with hand fatigue. There are colored handle bar ends to match your motorcycles paint. There are speaker systems that mount on handlebars.

One of the most important accessories for any motorcycle is a simple tire repair kit, that either comes packaged with threaded $CO2$ cartridges, or a small pump to inflate your tire. You never know when you will be in the middle of nowhere with a flat tire. Best to always be prepared, like the boy scouts!

The list of accessories is endless. You just have to do the research to discover the possibilities. If you have a need for something for your motorcycle, chances are it's already out there on the market!

Chapter Twenty Seven

Maintenance. It is a word that drives daggers of fear into the heart of just about any motorcyclist. But it need not be feared. Yearly maintenance of any motorcycle is something that can be done in one day in most cases.

What is yearly maintenance, and more importantly, what does it consist of? Well let's start with the basics. First things first. Buy a manual. I recommend a good aftermarket (There are many aftermarket manual; companies out there, Haynes and Clymer being the most popular) manual, which speaks to you in plain terms and makes working on your bike understandable, as opposed to the factory shop manuals, which are aimed and written at the seasoned mechanic.

An oil change in the spring is a good thing to do, especially if your motorcycle is not used for an extended period of time during the winter. If you start or ride your motorcycle once every two weeks or so in the cold months, then the oil change is only necessary if you have the amount of mileage you normally go through between changes. If you let it sit a month or so between start-ups then change that oil at the beginning of each season, as acid develops from sitting.

Next, take out your handy dandy cable-lubing tool (Any motorcycle dealer or catalogue, online sales store will have these available.) and lube all your cables on your motorcycle at the start of every season.

Next, move over to your brake system, and bleed all your motorcycles brake lines. Use only new unopened brake fluid from a fresh container (Brake fluid absorbs moisture from the air, so any opened containers that are not tightly sealed will naturally become contaminated with moisture.) So throw out old half empty containers and buy only a new container every year to bleed your brakes out with. Make sure you get the correct type of brake fluid. There are DOT 3 and 4, which are compatible and interchangeable. Then there is DOT 5, which is not compatible with anything else. It is silicone based, and cannot be used with any other type of brake fluid, because it will lead to brake failure. This is NOT a good thing! Check your motorcycle's manual or the aforementioned repair manual to get information on which fluid you will need.

One quick tip here: There are several products out there that make bleeding brakes easy, instead of a two man operation that is annoying. I use a product called "Speed bleeders" (http://www.speedbleeder.com) which are basically your typical brake bleeder valves, but with a not so typical one way check valve built in. So you squeeze your lever, the air goes out, you release, and that's it. Repeat until all the air is completely out of the system. You can also purchase a brake bleeding pump which will essentially do the same thing.

Next, fill your tires to the proper air pressure, as described by your manufacturer. There is usually a tag on the swing arm that states all of this information.

Now get out your handy inspection mirror and check your brake pads, to see how much life you have left in them. If needed, change them. This is usually a very easy endeavor that doesn't take too long to do at all.

Next comes the big stuff. These items may have to be completed by a mechanic, but they are something that any back yard mechanic with enough guts and especially know-how can accomplish easily enough.

Yearly valve adjustments. Most manufacturers vary in their need for valve adjustments in anywhere from 6,000 miles to 30,000 miles, depending on the motorcycle. If you do not ride as often as some, and your motorcycle requires, say 30,000 miles between adjustments, there's a good chance you may never need to have your valves adjusted.

But there are also those manufacturers who require valve adjustments every 6,000 miles. If you ride 20,000 miles a year, that's three adjustments you'll need to complete in the course of a year!

Another reason to thoroughly investigate any motorcycle you intend to purchase. If you are going to be a "Long Rider" then buy a motorcycle with ease of maintenance, coupled with long valve train adjustment intervals. What do I mean by "ease of maintenance"? Make sure there is as little to remove as possible to get under the gas tank, to where the engine and carburetor access is.

Speaking of carburetors, if you have a bank of these on your motorcycle (Some motorcycles are manufactured with fuel injection, and more and more of them are being manufactured that way every year now. Soon carbureted motorcycles will be a thing of the past!) You will need at least yearly carburetor synching done. This sounds daunting, but is actually very easy to do. There are many different carb synch gauges out there on the market. They range anywhere from about twenty dollars to well over a hundred or even more in some cases.

Next, it's time to install a fresh set of spark plugs. Buy the required plugs for your bike and set the gap before you begin to disassemble your motorcycle.

Now it's time to go around your motorcycle and look for things like frayed cables and dry rotting hoses. If you see any of this, replace those items immediately. There's no point in getting stuck somewhere because of little things like this.

All of these little things ad up to a nice, trouble free riding season.

If you're going to have a mechanic do all your work, then none of the above matters. But you would be surprised at the ease of performing most of this kind of work. Doing it for the first time is the trick. Once you get past that first hurdle, subsequent attempts are far easier.

Chapter Twenty Eight

We've spoken of spring maintenance, but what about winter maintenance? Didn't think you had to do winter maintenance? Just thought you'd put the bike away with an old tarp over it till the spring and call it a day?

Well guess again. Winter maintenance is easy, much more so than its spring counterpart. It requires you purchasing a "Float type Smart" battery charger. Which regulates itself, once a battery is charged to the proper level, and installing the leads for that charger to your battery. These type of motorcycle specific chargers come with a small harness that hooks up to your battery, and has a plug that connects to the battery charger, voiding the need to remove plastic bodywork every time you want to charge the battery.

Simply plug your battery's harness into that of the one on the charger, and your battery is being maintained all winter long.

Next, before you put the motorcycle away for the season, give it a good bath and polishing. A fresh coat of polish goes a long way towards making that bikes surface protected over the cold winter months.

After this, change the oil, this oil is just going to be left in the motorcycle for the winter months and will be dumped again in the spring, so leave your old filter on. The point is you'll be storing your bike with fresh oil without petroleum bi-products created from the engines running and dumping its carbons and such into the oil. Also, as we mentioned in the spring chapter, oil that sits to long can build up acids, which will scar your cylinder walls and valve train in the long run. So throw a fresh oil change in there, and the oil doesn't have to be anything fancy, just regular old SG certified automotive oil for the winter is fine. You're going to dump it all out in the spring anyway. The point of all this is to keep the engines internals acid free.

Do you ride in the winter? Then you don't have to do this. Just make sure you ride the motorcycle at least once every two weeks and ride it for at least 10-20 miles. That alone will keep the acids out of your system. If you go longer than that between startups, you're risking trouble.

Now for the most important part of winter maintenance. Stabilizing your fuel. Go out and buy a bottle of fuel stabilizer. Read the directions and then add the correct amount to your motorcycles gas tank, just before you fill it up. In other words, run your tank down low, Go to a gas station with your fuel stabilizer in hand (Or tank bag!) and add it to the near empty tank in the required amount for your gas tank size.

Now go for a nice 10 mile ride to help the stabilizer circulate and mix with your gas.

Why should you add fuel stabilizer? Gasoline goes bad when it sits. It forms gums and varnishes. These clog up your carburetors, and come springtime, you won't be able to start your motorcycle. You'll end up having to have your carburetor's acid bathed at least to clean them up and rid them of the gunk that has developed in them over a winter of sitting unused.

So by stabilizing the gas, you will save

yourself a decent amount of money in repairs, which can be put towards riding gear or motel rooms or food or more gadgets for your favorite motorcycle.

The last thing you should do to prepare for the cold months is to fill your motorcycles tires before putting her away. Fill them both to the manufacturer's recommendations, and then ride the motorcycle home and put a motorcycle cover on her, so that dust doesn't cover your precious motorcycle when you're out doing whatever it is you do in the winter months. You'll be happy you did come the spring.

Chapter Twenty Nine

Motorcycle rallies are a huge part of motorcycling. All across America, come June, July, August and September, rallies and events begin to pop up. So plan accordingly.

The first of these every year takes place in February in Daytona, Florida. Daytona Bike week is a week of raucous behavior that culminates in the start of the AMA racing season with the Daytona 200 race. Daytona is a HUGE "Biker" event with things like Coleslaw wrestling and wet T-shirt contests going on. There is also an area for sport bike riders where they can perform stunts and such. Daytona's official web site is www.daytonachamber.com.

Come the first full week in June. The Americade rally sprawls out across the Lake George, New York area. This is by far, my favorite event of every year. There are seminars by motorcycling luminaries all week long, as well as planned rides into the northern Adirondacks, Vermont, and the surrounding areas. Some of these rides are covered bridge tours, others tour the reservoirs in the area, and others are purely back road excursions. Americade also is the home of the Tour Expo center which is a flea market type sales area where you can purchase, and have installed just about anything for your motorcycle you could ever want. Need tires? Have them installed right at Americade's tour expo.

There are also nightly rodeos, and steam boat rides on Lake George. There are bike judging contests for cleanest, shiniest bikes as well as paint jobs, and accessories. There is the Great Escape amusement park nearby that has fireworks and other events for the rally. There are tons of things to do that first week in June at Americade.

What is the best part of Americade for me? The demo rides on just about every new motorcycle manufactured on the planet. Aprilia, BMW, Harley, Honda, Kawasaki, Moto Guzzi, Suzuki, Triumph, and Yamaha all set up demo rides at Americade every year.

The Americade event itself is very family oriented and lots of fun to do with a big group of friends. If you get bored at Americade, then there's no hope for you. The Internet web site for Americade is www.tourexpo.com.

The week after Americade is another event,

though this one is not family oriented, and is more a biker event, The Laconia, New Hampshire rally and ride. This is another event on the par with Americade, size-wise. Like Daytona bike week, this culminates in racing, this time at Louden racecourse, mere miles from Laconia. There are burnout pits with smoking tires and screaming engines along with loud debauchery on a nightly basis. Laconia's web address is www.laconiamcweek.com.

Another big event in June is the Honda Hoot. The Hoot is an all make event that has grown into something quite large. It is held in the south, usually in Tennessee, and is another very nice, family oriented event. There are rides into the nearby mountains and excursions into Dollywood, Dolly Parton's amusement park nearby. Like Americade, all the major manufacturers are there with demo fleets for your testing pleasure. This is another first class event with lots to do for the sport touring/touring rider. The Honda hoots web site is appropriately enough www.hondahoot.com.

Every July, the Gold wing riders hold their own event, called appropriately enough "Wing Ding". Wing Ding moves around the country each year, and is one of the best run, orderly events out there. They have bike judging contests as well as a huge flea market type are where you can buy all kinds of accessories for your motorcycle. (Primarily Gold wing accessories.) Wing Ding's web site is www.wing-ding.org.

Each July, The AMA hosts the Vintage Motorcycle day's race and rally in Mid-Ohio race complex. This is an event that boasts many race bikes from years gone by. It's an interesting and exciting rally with a different taste then most of the others. Go to AMAdirectlink.com to get the lowdown on the Vintage motorcycle day's event.

Come August, the biggest "Biker" event of the year comes around. The Sturgis rally in the Black Hills of South Dakota. This event is the big one for cruiser riders. It is one week of wild events in the foot hills that boasts attendance of about 250,000. This is a huge event. There are music concerts held almost daily from top name acts of the past, as well as some of the present day. All sorts of attractions abound at Sturgis, for the "Wild one" type of rider. Sturgis's web address is www.sturgis-rally.com.

In early September, the weekend after Labor Day, is the Killington Classic Rally. The Killington Classic is a fairly new event that book marks the summer nicely with Americade at the beginning and this event at the end. The Classic is held in Rutland, Vermont near the Killington ski resort. The event is young, but so far shows great promise, and should be a fantastic event in a few short years. It's already great fun now. Go to www.killingtonclassic.com to learn more about the Classic.

In October, the riding year culminates in a return to Daytona for Biketoberfest. A fairly new event that wraps up the season nicely. Smaller than Daytona bike week, Biketoberfest is a lower key rally then some of the other "Biker" events. Biketoberfest information can be found at www.biktoberfest.org.

The AMA hosts and sponsors motorcycle racing as one of their major attractions each year.

They have massive series in several different classes across the country with a whole slate of events at each track. Superbike, Super sport, Super stock, formula extreme, all levels of dirt bike racing, both indoor and outdoor, the list is almost endless. They even offer flat track racing. Go to a race this year and be amazed at the skill level of the professional rider. Racing is a thrilling event every motorcyclist can enjoy.

There are many smaller events throughout the year. Some are brand or even model oriented. The ones listed above are the major events you'll find of each year.

Chapter Thirty

Clubs are a large part of motorcycling enjoyment. There are many types of clubs and organizations out there.

The Kawasaki Good Times Owners Club is a great organization that has hospitality areas set up at most major events where you can park your motorcycle in their private parking area, as well as be treated to free refreshments and get first dibs on the next day's demo rides. The GTOC membership also includes a towing package for every motorcycle you own. You also get a $50 reimbursement coupon good at Kawasaki dealerships towards accessories if you take a Motorcycle Safety Foundation (MSF) course. The best part is that it only costs about $35 per year to belong, and you don't have to own a Kawasaki to be a member. You can find the GTOC's online information at http://www.kawasaki.com/gtoc/main.html.

The American Motorcyclists Association was mentioned briefly earlier in this tome. They are an organization that fight for motorcyclist's rights against every other entity that seeks to take our riding rights away, one small chunk at a time. You can check them out at www.amadirectlink.org.

Honda has their own club called the Honda Rider's club of America. Included is a roadside assistance program, a towing program, a 24 hr., 7 day a week weather service, lost key replacement and a magazine. Their club runs about $40 per year and, like the Kawasaki club, has much to offer. Though I believe you must own a Honda motorcycle to belong to this one. The address to get the lowdown on the Honda rider's club is www.hrca.honda.com.

Suzuki has their own club as well, though the Suzuki Owners Club is more of a grass roots effort than anything else, as it is member run and created without any help from Suzuki whatsoever. The club has a newsletter, and runs events every year. The yearly membership fee is only $10. The Suzuki Owners club address is www.soc-usa.org.

Harley owners also have their own club called HOG, or Harley Owners Group. You can find information about HOG at www.harley-davidson.com/ex/hog.

These are the major clubs for motorcyclists. There are many smaller clubs across the country. Search the Internet for references to others in your area.

Chapter Thirty One

One of the largest events each and every year are the new International motorcycle shows held across the nation. These are large events that house every manufacturer and quite a few aftermarket parts companies in huge convention centers such as the Javitts center in New York City. The San Mateo county expo center in San Francisco, The Cobb Galleria in Atlanta and many more.

Manufacturers such as Yamaha, Kawasaki, Honda, Suzuki, Harley, BMW, Moto Guzzi, Aprilia, Ducati and many more fill the convention centers with eye candy for the winter starved riding community. Every new motorcycle each manufacturer produces is on display so you can sit, touch and just get a general idea of how each and every motorcycle feels under you.

All the latest innovations are present for you to look at first hand. Have a question about a new motorcycle you saw in this month's magazine? Now is the time to ask it of the well-versed staffers who mill about each and every display.

Some manufacturers even have accessories displayed prominently nearby.

There is even entertainment on hand, such as trials bikes ridden by some top notch and exceptional riders who perform all sorts of amazing tricks before your very eyes!

Looking for a certain riding boot? Or electric clothing? Or even the lowdown on an upcoming rally for the new season? The information will be in the vendor's area of each show. Many of the prominent magazines will have their booths set up to sell subscriptions as well, you can get just about everything you'll ever need for a motorcycle at these shows, including information!

Go to http://show.motorcycleshows.com on the World Wide Web for more information on the shows near you.

Chapter Thirty Two

Now it is time for putting it all together. What does that mean? It means it's time to take all the knowledge and tips in this book and apply them to the real world.

Do you remember what "The Stagger" is? It's when we ride with other motorcycles and stagger the motorcycles a second apart in opposite car tracks and two seconds apart in the same car track.

What about "The Scan?" Do you remember what the scan is? It's when we are riding; we check both mirrors as well as ahead of us continually every few seconds, scanning twelve seconds around us. We use all quick looks with a quick return to the front to identify whatever dangers may exist around us.

How about "The Count"? You remember that? That is the process we take when counting seconds behind other vehicles. Two seconds behind vehicles directly ahead of us, one second behind a staggered motorcycle in the other tire track. We use a reference point of either a signpost, a section of the dotted line, or even a pothole the vehicle in front of us just passed over. Count in your head "One thousand and one, one thousand and two" and that's where you should be.

What's the most important thing to remember concerning motorcycling? It's to ride your own ride. Don't be so involved with the group mentality of others that you end up riding to and above your limits. Always ride with your head, not your ego. Remember this, always, riding on the street you should not exceed 70% of your ability. Always leave

30% in check.

You remember our discussion about being courteous to other drivers, and not presenting yourself on a motorcycle as someone others would fear or become annoyed with, correct?

Don't forget about looking through a turn to its end and placing your line there. Always look as far ahead in a turn as you can see. Where you stare equals what? Where you and your motorcycle will end up. Remember the twelve-second rule.

What about the proper riding gear? What about the process of looking for the correct motorcycle for you and how to go about finalizing your choice? Do you remember the few simple parking lot maneuvers I laid out for you? How about the information I mentioned concerning accidents and how to go about emergency procedures?

Remember how to park your motorcycle? Nose facing up hill, not down, transmission in first gear, and the steering head locked.

How is the best way to make sure other motorists recognize you? Headlamp on high beam, extra reflective material or auxiliary rear lighting, and an aftermarket horn.

Re-read whatever sections you have to, to make sure all of this is ingrained in your mind.

I have tried throughout this book to give you insights and warnings of what can possibly happen to you on the road. The bottom line is you must be prepared for any eventuality, and you have to keep yourself, your mind and body, focused on what you are doing, and not day dreaming, or worrying about others with you. Let the lead and sweep riders keep track of everyone in between. If you are not one of these riders, then just enjoy your ride. As a novice rider, you should always be concerned about your riding and safety, and make it a constant point in your own mind.

As a seasoned rider, we all could use reminders and refreshers along the way. Motorcycling is a complex and enjoyable sport that is riddled with naysayers and detractors in one form or another. Always try to put forward the best image you can as a motorcyclist. You'll help more than just yourself; you'll help all of us.

Relax when riding, eventually all of this will be second nature and you'll be performing each and every one of these procedures without thinking about it. Riding a motorcycle is meant to be fun, but you have to get through the learning curve before that can truly happen. It's very easy to get overwhelmed by it all and become awed by the whole experience of riding. The view is different from the seat of a motorcycle, then from inside a steel and glass cage. When something makes you want to stop and stare at it, do that. Stop and stare at whatever it is, be it a mountain vista or a distant cloud cover, or even a reflective cityscape. There's nothing wrong with pulling to the side of a road and taking a look at the world, instead of simply blowing through it. The trick is realizing when and where to pull over. Eventually all of this will come as second nature, and with enough practice in the beginning you'll be using every one of these techniques all the time, without realizing it, and that's the way it's meant to be.

So get out there and start putting these tips and tricks to use. Every technique outlined here will make your riding experience a far better, and most importantly a far safer one. Motorcycling is not a haphazard skill that anyone can get right by simply jumping on a motorcycle and thundering off. It takes years of practice, and in truth there is a constant, never ending learning curve. But by putting these techniques outlined here to use every day, you can shorten that learning curve quicker, making motorcycling a practice of fun! Now get out there and ride your motorcycle. The more miles you put under your two wheels, the better you'll become, but only if you ride smart, and only if you ride like they're all out to get you!

Appendix

This is a list of links to motorcycle relevant websites on the Internet.

Manufacturers Sites: On each of these pages you can see each manufacturer's offerings of new motorcycles for each new model year.

Aprilia: http://www.aprilia.com

BMW: http://www.bike.bmw.com/english/index.html

Ducati: http://www.ducati.com/

Harley Davidson: http://www.harley-davidson.com/

Honda: http://www.hondamotorcycle.com/

Kawasaki: http://www.kawasaki.com/index.html

Moto Guzzi: http://motoguzzi.com/

MuZ: http://www.motorradna.com/

Suzuki: http://www.suzukicycles.com/

Triumph: http://www.triumph.co.uk/usa/

Yamaha: http://yamaha-motor.com

News and information sites: These websites are chock full of Internet related motorcycle news on a daily basis.

Motorcycle Daily:
http://www.motorcycledaily.com/
An excellent daily website that always has relevant motorcycle information updated on a daily basis.

Motorcycle Online: http://motorcycle.com
A very good online magazine that has reviews of both motorcycles and riding gear. An excellent resource.

Motorcycle World: http://motorcycleworld.com/

Rider Report:
http://www.riderreport.com//index.cfm? Rider Magazines home on the web for their entire family of magazines.

Bikez.com: http://bikez.com/
An Internet web site that lists all sorts of useful multi-brand information.

Beginner Bikes:
http://www.beginnerbikes.com/index.html
A web site with information pertaining to only beginner motorcycles for the new rider. A VERY good resource.

Motorcyclist Magazine:
http://www.motorcyclistonline.com/
The online home of one of the premiere motorcycle

magazines on the newsstands.

Cycle World magazine:
http://www.cycleworld.com/
The Internet version of another popular and excellent motorcycle magazine.

Motorcycle Consumer News:
http://www.mcnews.com the premiere no-adds magazine for motorcyclists. This magazine tells it like it is and does not accept advertisements from anyone. So you know you are getting the straight truth about a product or motorcycle.

Organizations:

The American Motorcyclists Association (The AMA): www.amadirectlink.org.
The World Wide Web link for the only motorcyclists rights group in the United States.

The Motorcycle Safety Foundation (MSF):
http://www.msf-usa.org/
The MSF offers rider safety course nationwide that are the standard for all aspects of riding safe in this country.

The Snell Memorial Foundation (Snell):
http://www.smf.org/
The testing organization that has the most stringent motorcycle test standards for helmets.

Mail order parts suppliers:
Below is a list of mail order parts houses on the Internet. You'll find the most variety and information on their web sites for whatever your need is for your motorcycle. I am not endorsing or detracting from any of these suppliers, I am only giving you the option of knowing what is out there. I will say that I have used every site I am placing in this index at one time or another.

Chaparral motorsports:
http://www.chaparral-racing.com/
Chaparral is one of the largest dealers on the web, offering parts and accessories from just about every manufacturer, both aftermarket and original equipment out there.

Competition Accessories:
http://www.competitionaccessories.com/
Competition Accessories, or "Comp A" as they are called by some, is another large mail order Company that offers a large selection of goods at reasonable prices.

Motorcycle Accessory Warehouse:
http://www.accwhse.com/
MAW is another good alternative when shopping for motorcycle parts and accessories. They ship from several different warehouses across the country.

Southwest Moto Tires:
http://www.swmototires.com/
A motorcycle tire only store

California sport Touring:
http://www.casporttouring.com/
A fairly new company that has some excellent prices and is worth looking into.

Kneedraggers.com:
http://kneedraggers.com/
A sportier oriented that has a large selection and easy to use menus. Worth checking out.

Parts 411:
http://www.parts411.com/
Another sport bike site that offers a wide selection of products.

Ron Ayers:
http://www.ronayers.com/main.cfm
Ron Ayers is a dealership in the Southeast that offers great prices and excellent service.

The Helmet Shop:
http://www.helmetshop.com
A helmet only store that specializes in the best brands and helmet related products out there.

Ralph L. Angelo, Jr.

Final thoughts

What final thoughts can I impart to you all? This book is first and foremost a "How to ride a motorcycle safely" book. But it has its other sides as well. There are sections here that show the fun side of motorcycling such as the accessorizing and the great road trips you can have with friends and family.

Do yourself a favor, read other books as well about our sport, especially books by Keith Code and David L. Hough. These guys are the gurus of riding. Subscribe to a few magazines about motorcycling. Immerse yourself in the sport. It will take control of you and pull you in. You will love riding on two wheels, or you will find it's not for you. But if you've gotten this far, then I believe you're already hooked.

One last item I ask of you all. Go rent a DVD called "Faster" It is the account of the 2001 & 2002 Moto GP seasons. Watch the movie from end to end, it's literally one hour and forty minutes out of your life. But pay special attention to the words of Kevin Schwantz at the very end when the credits are rolling. Then watch and listen to the words of everyone else they talk to in the closing credits.

To a man they say one thing. The Street is not the place to ride fast. If you want to ride fast, do it on a track.

Rent this great DVD, it's well worth it and it's enjoyable as well as sobering. Riding a motorcycle should be fun. When you have guys like Valentino Rossi and John Hopkins showing how much fun it can be with such great youthful enthusiasm, it can easily be understood why so many love our sport. Because they've learned how much fun it is, and can continue to be well into the latter years of one's life.

It's also understandable how so many consider riding a motorcycle to be a dangerous and frightening hobby as well.

But for those of us who know better, who have learned to ride like "They're all out to get me!" we know the secrets of riding for many years to come, and for doing it safely.

God Bless! May you put 200,000 infinitely enjoyable miles in the next ten years on your two wheeled wonders, and most importantly, may you do it safely!

Ralph

Ralph L. Angelo, Jr.

www.ingramcontent.com/pod-product-compliance
Lightning Source LLC
Chambersburg PA
CBHW061648040426
42446CB00010B/1641